Tropical Asian Cooking

Published by Periplus Editions with editorial offices at
130 Joo Seng Road #06-01, Olivine Building, Singapore 368357.

ISBN: 0-7946-0006-9 (paperback)
ISBN: 0-7946-0083-2 (hardcover)
Library of Congress Control Number: 2001096483

Distributed by
North America
Tuttle Publishing, 364 Innovation Drive
North Clarendon, VT 05759-9436, USA
Tel (802) 773-8930; fax (802) 773-6993

Asia Pacific
Berkeley Books Pte Ltd, 130 Joo Seng Road #06-01
Olivine Building, Singapore 368357
Tel (65) 280-1330; fax (65) 280-6290

Japan and Korea
Tuttle Publishing, RK Building 2nd Floor
2-13-10 Shimo Meguro, Meguro-Ku, Tokyo 153 0064, Japan
Tel (81-3) 5437-0171; fax (81-3) 5437-0755

Indonesia
PT Java Books Indonesia, Jl. Kelapa Gading Kirana
Blok A14 No. 17, Jakarta 14240, Indonesia
Tel (62-21) 451 5351; fax (62-21) 453 4987

PRINTED IN SINGAPORE

Tropical Asian Cooking

Exotic Flavors from Equatorial Asia

recipes by Four Seasons Hotels
photography by Masano Kawana
styling by Christina Ong
text by Wendy Hutton

PERIPLUS

contents

Whether it's an early breakfast or a mid-morning brunch taken after that first exhilarating dip in the sea or swimming pool, the fresh beauty of a tropical morning deserves to be celebrated at the table. Wake up to refreshing ideas for tropical smoothies, cereals, jams, Chinese omelets, Indian pancakes, congee, and Indonesian deep-fried bananas.

In the warmth of the midday sun, think light bites, spicy salads, and cooling sweets. Be inspired by noodles—both fried and bathed in broth—by delicate, tropical soups, steamed fish, and lightly poached, fragrant poultry dishes. Finally, cool off with coconut, palm honey, and pandan ice creams or stretch out below a whirling ceiling fan and embrace the afternoon with a slice of sublime passionfruit cheese cake.

The freshness that comes with the evening sharpens the appetite. There is plenty of time to spend on the preparation and leisurely enjoyment of food that celebrates the end of a wonderful day. Fish dishes run the gamut from grilled and simmered snapper to spiced tuna steak with citrus salsa. Have tiger prawns served with a *vindaloo* dip, or opt for the ultimate in spicy seafood: Singapore's famous chili crab. For meat lovers there is Vietnamese beef, fragrant coriander steak, beef with *rendang* marinade, and *tandoori* lamb.

Decorate your table and garden for a special alfresco party and delight guests with scented candles, tropical orchids, and colorful table throws against a backdrop of haunting *gamelan*, funky *tabla*, or Asian jazz fusion. Finger-food is the name of the game when it comes to casual entertaining. Enjoy spring rolls, *chapati* wraps, succulent satay, Balinese sushi, Asian pizza, and Chinese pot-stickers, and to cap it all … banana, chocolate, and fresh mint samosa!

foreword by
nobuyuki matsuhisa

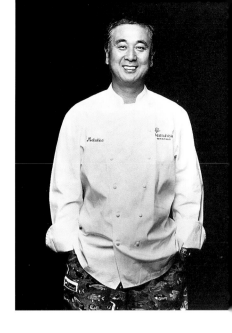

This book truly represents the contemporary flavors of tropical South and Southeast Asia today. It is unashamedly Asian without being traditional—reflecting the fascinating blend of peoples and cultures found in the region. What is particularly fascinating to me is the interaction between the cuisines—the new combinations that arise, combining and yet preserving the distinctive character and strength of the indigenous dishes and ingredients.

This modern, fresh approach to Asian cooking is the kind of food I love—honest food that is easy to put together and guaranteed to please. I have been fortunate to cook at several of the Four Seasons hotels throughout Asia, swapping tips with chefs who hail from every corner of the region. Herewith are presented a selection of their best recipes that are absolutely perfect for every occasion—from a simple breakfast for two, to an alfresco picnic or barbecue, to an elegant dinner party with friends at home.

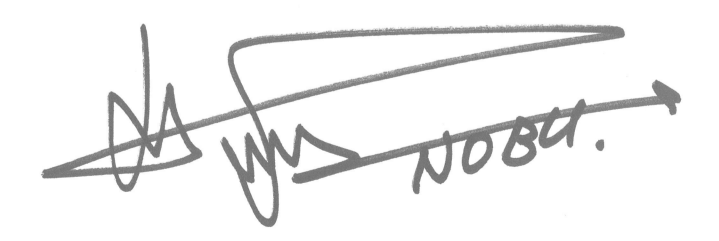

NOBU.

Entrance to Four Seasons Resort Bali at Sayan

dining in the tropics

Lands where soft tropical breezes carry a hint of spices and scented flowers, where warm seas bathe coral reefs teeming with fish, where life-giving monsoon rains nourish an endless variety of lush fruit, vegetables, and intensely aromatic herbs … who has not dreamed of tropical Asia, and longed to experience its sensuous beauty?

Fortunately, it's not essential to travel to enjoy the exquisite flavors of some of the world's most exciting and creative cuisines, encapsulating all that is magical in these exotic lands. Try any of the recipes within these pages and you're already halfway there.

For centuries, some of the most precious produce of the region has been sought by the West: pepper and cardamom from India, nutmeg and cloves from Indonesia's Spice Islands, cinnamon from Sri Lanka, and galangal from mainland Southeast Asia. Today, there's a lot more than spices on supermarket shelves. Thanks to increased international travel, and to migration and the consequent opening of ethnic restaurants, Asian markets, and specialty shops, the diverse flavors of tropical Asia can be recreated in kitchens around the world.

This collection of recipes includes the major cuisines of tropical Asia. While some classic dishes are included, most incorporate a new approach to the region's cuisines. No longer confined by tradition or isolated by limited communications, Asian cooks are happily borrowing the cooking styles and ingredients of their neighbors, or from even further afield. Many traditional dishes have been modified for a fresher, lighter taste, adapted to suit today's health-conscious gourmets.

Luxurious hotels in tropical Asia — such as the highly esteemed Four Seasons properties — have been at the forefront of the evolution of the "new" tropical cuisine. Their chefs come from a wide range of backgrounds, and their sharing of knowledge and experience has led to exciting adapations and variations. A Balinese may work together with a Swiss who happens to have spent time in Tokyo to create new types of sushi; a Singaporean chef and his Thai colleague may jointly create a new twist to a classic laksa noodle soup; a Maldivian chef may discuss with his French counterpart how to improve a traditional vegetable curry, or decide to use olive oil rather than saturated coconut oil. In this collection of fabulous recipes, chefs of Four Seasons properties around the region share with us just such recipes which have been carefully adapted for use in the home kitchen.

The recipes featured in this book are inspired by the cuisines of tropical India; of the Indian Ocean archipelago of the Maldives; the islands of Indonesia and Singapore, and — on the Southeast Asian mainland — Malaysia, Thailand, and Vietnam.

Tropical central and southern India have produced a style of cooking that has not only spread into nearby countries such as the Maldives, but which has traveled with Indian migrants as far as Singapore and Malaysia. Yet the influence has not been one way, for centuries earlier, some of the spices of Indonesia's Moluccan islands — especially cloves, nutmeg, and mace — found their way into Indian spice chests.

Apart from the liberal use of spices, the food of India and the Maldives is often pungent with chilies, although their heat is frequently soothed by the rich coconut milk added to gravies and sauces. Yogurt, too, adds a cooling touch to sides, salads, and drinks.

Tropical seasonings not found in cooler regions of India — including the inimitable curry leaves and pungent brown mustard seeds — add a distinctive note to many dishes. Borrowed from northern India, widely popular seasoning mixes or *masala* such as the spicy flavorings of *tandoori* food are quite happily incorporated into tropical-style grills.

Surrounded by the warm waters of the Indian Ocean, the inhabitants of the Maldives naturally enjoy fish as their major source of protein. This appears in many guises, such as fish curry with pineapple and coconut milk; grilled fish cubes marinated in *tandoori* spices; pan-fried fish cakes with a herb-laden curry dip; and grilled tiger prawns with a typical *vindaloo* sauce from Goa.

The major cuisines of Southeast Asia — Thai, Vietnamese, Malaysian, Singaporean, and Indonesian — have all been influenced to varying degrees by the culinary genius of China. Ingredients such as noodles, tofu (bean curd), soy sauce, and fresh bean sprouts are just some Chinese ingredients found in almost all of tropical Asia.

Ketchumbar salad; Grilled fish *tikka* in pandan leaf

Tempura oysters with hot sauce; Wok-fried clams with chili and Chinese sausage; Soft-shelled crab with chili dip; Raw fish salad with flavored oil

In addition to a wide range of Chinese seasonings and local spices and herbs, the food of most of tropical Asia is full of aromatic roots and members of the onion family (onions, garlic, shallots, scallions). The huge botanical family of gingers includes many edible varieties, including the common ginger known throughout the world. Brilliant yellow turmeric, galangal (used medicinally in Europe in the Middle Ages), camphor-scented aromatic ginger, and the edible pink bud of another wild ginger are all used fresh, their intense flavor adding to regional cuisines.

Singapore, a tiny but vibrant metropolis just north of the equator and off the southern tip of the Malay Peninsula, is largely populated by ethnic Chinese. In addition to its wide array of southern Chinese dishes, Singapore offers the food of its indigenous Malays, and the flavors of the Indian Subcontinent brought by 19th-century migrants. If there has to be one place in all of tropical Asia where it is possible to enjoy both traditional and creative new dishes from the entire region, it is Singapore. Often well traveled and, for the most part, familiar with international cuisine,

Singapore's chefs have actively worked at evolving a new pan-Asian cuisine based on the wide range of local dishes already found in the country. It's not just East meets West, but East meets East in Singapore, where the philosophy seems to be "if an ingredient works, it doesn't matter where it's from, just use it."

The creation of a cross-cultural cuisine is nothing new for Singapore. More than a century ago, the blending of Chinese and Malay cultures and cuisines in Singapore and the Malaysian centers of Malacca (Melaka) and Penang (Pulau Pinang) led to the evolution of what is known locally as Nonya food. This clever blending of Chinese ingredients and cooking styles with the local spices, herbs, and fruits is without doubt one of tropical Asia's finest culinary offerings.

The cuisine of Malaysia (where the major races are Malay, Chinese, and Indian) shares much with neighboring Singapore and with Indonesia. Both Malay and Indonesian food (particularly that of Sumatra) are robustly spiced and enlivened with chilies. Large fresh red or green chilies,

dried chilies, and tiny fiery fresh chilies known as bird's-eye chilies all have their individual flavor, fragrance, and color, and are used accordingly.

Of all the Indonesian islands, it is Bali that has most enchanted the world. With its incredible physical beauty and unique culture that is an integral part of daily life and not just something paraded for tourists, Bali is also home to a distinctive cuisine. And because some of its chefs — like the tourists — come from around the world to work side-by-side with Balinese chefs, Bali has become another center where a creative new cuisine based on traditional dishes is evolving.

Many of the fresh herbs which enhance the food of Malaysia and Indonesia also add their almost head-spinning aroma to the food of Thailand and Vietnam. Redolent of the jungle, they include lemongrass, kaffir lime leaf, Indonesian *salam* leaf, a range of basils, fresh cilantro, regular mint, long-stemmed or "Vietnamese mint," and fragrant pandan leaves.

The cuisine of Thailand and Vietnam is admired throughout tropical Asia, and some of its most distinctive ingredients, such as salty, pungent fish sauce, are borrowed by neighboring cooks. Thailand has several different regional cuisines but, overall, the food can be described as intensely flavorful. It is often hot, yet mild dishes soothed by coconut milk or reflecting Chinese origins can also be found. Lovers of fresh vegetables, the Thais are masters at producing superb salads. In Vietnam, salads may consist of a large platter of fresh herbs which are eaten together with cooked food ranging from fresh or deep-fried spring rolls to grilled meats. Less spicy than the cuisine of Thailand, Vietnamese food is generally fragrant, sometimes slightly sweet, and as it is rarely deep-fried — ideal for health-conscious food lovers.

To discover more of the fresh new flavors of tropical Asia, turn the pages of this book, choose a recipe or two, visit your nearest Asian market, then start cooking. Decorate your table with a piece of *batik* cloth or a *sari*, scatter it with orchids or perfumed flowers, put on a CD of haunting *gamelan* music, light an incense stick, and enjoy the sensations of tropical Asia.

Tandoori lobster; Henry the heron enjoys a morning stroll; Resort fishermen display their catch—Maldives

tropical morning

A tropical dawn. Perfectly still, perfectly silent. The breeze has not yet begun ruffling the coconut fronds, and the sun is just beginning to run silver fingers over the calm sea. Then the strident call of a kingfisher signals the full arrival of the day. Responding to the wake-up call, other birds start to warble and whistle, insects begin their gentle hum, and thoughts turn slowly to breakfast.   Whether it's an early breakfast or a mid-morning brunch taken after that first refreshing dip in the sea or swimming pool, the fresh beauty of a tropical morning deserves to be celebrated at the table. A positive cornucopia of tropical fruits — pineapple, mango, papaya, guava, starfruit, bananas, rambutan, and *salak* (snake fruit) to name just a few — is there to enjoy. Try your fruit blended with yogurt as a smoothie or *lassi*, or turn your tropical fruit into a simple jam, flavored with local herbs and spices such as lemongrass, cinnamon, and star anise. Instead of regular cereal, why not enjoy Bali's glutinous black rice, made into a type of sweet porridge and served with bananas with a hazelnut and chocolate filling? Still on the theme of rice, there's the wonderful savory rice porridge with Taiwan-style accompaniments. Alternatively, you might like to try Balinese-style muesli or a south Indian *masala dosai* (a potato-stuffed crispy pancake) to set you up for the day.   If you regard breakfast or brunch as incomplete without eggs, you could enjoy a succulent Chinese-style crab and asparagus omelet with pickles, or poached eggs on ham with a medley of vegetables and spicy hollandaise sauce.   Don't forget to add coffee (you could flavor it with cardamom pods or a stick of cinnamon), or try Asian green tea, simple and unadorned. Deliciously satisfied by your breakfast or brunch, the day is yours to enjoy.

Mango, fig, and date breakfast bar

8 oz (250 g) dried mango, chopped
12 oz (375 g) dried figs, chopped
8 oz (250 g) dried dates, pitted and
    chopped
1 1/4 cups (300 ml) vegetable oil
Scant 1 cup (250 g) honey
1/2 cup (125 g) soft brown sugar
8 eggs
1 teaspoon vanilla essence
1 orange
1 lemon
1 1/2 cups (435 g) all-purpose (plain)
    flour
1 3/4 cups (280 g) rolled oats
4 teaspoons baking powder
3 teaspoons cinnamon powder
2 1/2 teaspoons bicarbonate of soda
    (baking soda)
1 1/2 teaspoons salt

The warm fragrance of cinnamon permeates this mixture of dried fruits, citrus juice and zest, flour, oats, and honey. Make these in advance and store in an airtight container for serving at breakfast, or any time a delicious fruity snack is called for.

1 Preheat oven to 350°F (180°C, gas 4).
2 Place dried fruits in a bowl and add warm water to just cover the fruit. Soak for 5 minutes, then strain, discarding any liquid.
3 Whisk together the oil and honey in a bowl, then add sugar, eggs, and vanilla essence. Grate the orange and lemon to obtain the zest, then squeeze to obtain the juice. Add both lots of zest and juice to the bowl and whisk to combine.
4 Place flour, oats, baking and cinnamon powders, bicarbonate of soda, and salt in a large bowl, stirring to mix well. Add the dried fruits and honey mixture, stirring to combine.
5 Transfer the mixture into a small greased non-stick loaf pan, pressing down firmly with the back of a spoon. Bake at 350°F until set, about 30 minutes. Cool, turn out, then cut across into bars. Refrigerate in a covered container for up to one month.

Trio of tropical jams

Pineapple, vanilla, and star anise jam
3 1/2 teaspoons powdered pectin
1 cup (250 g) sugar
1 lb (500 g) finely diced fresh ripe
    pineapple
4 vanilla beans, split lengthways
1 whole star anise

Papaya, clove, and lemongrass jam
3 1/2 teaspoons powdered pectin
1 cup (250 g) sugar
1 lb (500 g) finely diced firm, ripe
    papaya
2 stems lemongrass, very finely
    chopped
1/4 cup (60 ml) lemon juice
1/2 teaspoon ground cloves

Rhubarb and nutmeg jam
3 1/2 teaspoons powdered pectin
1 cup (250 g) sugar
1 lb (500 g) finely diced rhubarb
1/2 teaspoon freshly grated nutmeg

Pineapple, vanilla, and star anise jam
1 Put pectin in a small bowl and stir in 1 tablespoon of the sugar. Set aside.
2 Place remaining sugar, pineapple, vanilla beans, and star anise in a saucepan and bring slowly to a boil, stirring constantly. Boil without stirring until mixture is thick, about 15 minutes, then add the pectin mix. Stir over low heat, 2 minutes, then remove from heat. Remove vanilla beans and star anise, then transfer jam to a sterilized glass jar.

Papaya, clove, and lemongrass jam
1 Put pectin in a small bowl and stir in 1 tablespoon of the sugar. Set aside.
2 Place remaining sugar, papaya, lemongrass, lemon juice, and cloves in a saucepan and bring slowly to a boil, stirring constantly. Boil without stirring until mixture is thick, about 15 minutes, then add the pectin mix. Stir over low heat, 2 minutes, then remove from heat and transfer to a sterilized glass jar.

Rhubarb and nutmeg jam
1 Put pectin in a small bowl and stir in 1 tablespoon of the sugar. Set aside.
2 Place remaining sugar, rhubarb, and nutmeg in a saucepan and bring slowly to a boil, stirring constantly. Boil without stirring until mixture is thick, about 15 minutes, then add the pectin mix. Stir over low heat, 2 minutes, then remove from heat and transfer to a sterilized glass jar.

Balinese tropical muesli

2 cups (200 g) rolled oats
2 medium apples, skin left on, grated
1 cup (200 g) finely diced fresh
  pineapple
1/4 cup (25 g) desiccated coconut
1/4 cup (40 g) raisins
1/4 cup (40 g) finely diced dried mango
1/4 cup (40 g) finely diced dried
  soursop or dried papaya
1/4 cup (50 g) finely diced dried apple
3 tablespoons honey
3–3 1/2 cups (750–875 ml) milk
Fresh mango slices to garnish

This muesli makes a nutritionally (and deliciously) complete meal. As almost all the ingredients are soaked overnight, all you'll need to do in the morning is stir and garnish the muesli—and make the coffee.

1 Combine oats, apples, pineapple, coconut, and dried fruits in a large bowl, stirring to mix well. Add the honey and 3 cups (750 ml) of the milk. Mix thoroughly, then cover bowl and refrigerate overnight.
2 In the morning, add more milk as required to achieve the desired consistency; cream or plain yogurt could be added instead of milk if preferred. Serve in glass bowls, garnished with the mango slices. You could also garnish this muesli with orange segments or strawberry slices.

Note: For maximum vitamins, add the fresh apple and pineapple in the morning, before adding extra milk to serve. The dried mango, soursop, or papaya could be replaced with other dried fruits such as apricot and peach.

Tropical smoothies

2 cups (500 ml) chilled skim milk
3/4 cup (185 ml) chilled plain yogurt
  (see recipe, page 32)
6 1/2 oz (200 g) mango, diced, or
  6 1/2 oz (200 g) puréed guava
1 1/2 teaspoons lime juice
4 tablespoons honey
4 ice cubes

Delicious and healthy mixtures of soft tropical fruits, skim milk, yogurt, lime juice, and honey make a great start to the day, and could also be enjoyed as a between-meal snack.

Combine all ingredients in a blender and process at high speed until smooth. Pour into four glasses and serve immediately.

Poolside breakfast at the villa —Four Seasons Resorts Bali

Chinese-style crab and asparagus omelet with vegetable pickle

8 eggs
4 oz (125 g) cooked crabmeat, picked over for any cartilage
1 cup (80 g) finely shredded long white Chinese (napa) cabbage
1/2 small onion, very thinly sliced
4 asparagus spears, thinly sliced
1/2 cup (40 g) finely shredded leek, or scallion (spring onion)
4 teaspoons cornstarch
1 teaspoon salt
1/4 teaspoon white pepper
2 tablespoons vegetable oil

Vegetable pickle
1 cup (250 ml) water
1/2 cup (125 ml) white vinegar
3 tablespoons sugar
1 tablespoon coarse salt
2/3 cup (75 g) carrot, finely julienned
1/3 cup (60 g) cucmber, skin left on, finely julienned
1/3 cup (45 g) red capsicum, finely julienned
2–3 shallots, thinly sliced

This omelet contains a delicate mixture of crabmeat, Chinese cabbage, and asparagus, with extra flavor coming from a little leek and onion. The secret is to shred or slice all the vegetables very finely, and to cook the omelet over moderate heat so the vegetables are just cooked by the time the egg has set.

1 To prepare the pickle, bring the water, vinegar, sugar, and salt to a boil in a small saucepan, stirring until the sugar and salt have dissolved. Put the prepared vegetables in a bowl and mix well by hand. Pour over the hot vinegar mix and leave to cool, then refrigerate 1–2 hours to chill thoroughly. (If you prefer a more crunchy version of this pickle, allow the vinegar mix to cool before pouring over the vegetables. If liked, you could add 1 shredded large red chili to the vegetables.)
2 To make the omelet, crack the eggs into a large bowl and beat lightly. Stir in the crabmeat, cabbage, onion, asparagus, leek, cornstarch, salt, and pepper, mix well.
3 Heat 1/2 tablespoon oil in a large non-stick skillet. Add half the omelet mixture, spreading it evenly round the pan. Cook over moderate heat, without stirring, until the egg is golden brown underneath and starting to set on top, about 3 minutes. Slide the omelet onto a plate. Add another 1/2 tablespoon oil to the pan and, when hot, reverse the plate to return omelet to the pan, with the cooked side facing up. Cook until done, another 2–3 minutes. Keep warm while repeating the method with the remaining ingredients.
4 Cut each omelet in half and transfer to 4 serving plates. Serve with vegetable pickle, or if liked, the omelet could be accompanied by some soy sauce, or fish sauce with sliced bird's-eye chilies.

Note: The vegetable pickle is best made 2–3 hours in advance to give time for chilling; if preferred, it could be made the day before. It will keep in a covered container in the refrigerator for up to one week.

Stirring the vegetables into the egg mixture

Poached eggs on ham and vegetable medley with spicy hollandaise sauce

3 tablespoons clarified butter (*ghee*) or vegetable oil
1 large onion, diced
8 oz (250 g) picnic ham, diced
2 cups (300 g) diced mixed vegetables, such as red bell pepper (capsicum), cassava (tapioca), potato, sweet potato, sweet corn kernels, green beans, and carrots
3 tablespoons finely chopped assorted fresh herbs, such as fresh cilantro (coriander), basil, and parsley
1/4 teaspoon salt
Freshly ground black pepper to taste
8 poached eggs (see Note)
4 slices French bread, toasted
Fresh parsley sprigs to garnish

Hollandaise sauce
2 egg yolks
Salt and white pepper to taste
1 tablespoon lemon juice
1 tablespoon white wine vinegar
2/3 cup (125 g) butter

Sweet chili *sambal*
1 tablespoon vegetable oil
5–6 large red chilies, sliced
1–2 bird's-eye chilies, sliced
4 cloves garlic, sliced
2 medium tomatoes, chopped
1/4 teaspoon dried shrimp paste
1/2 teaspoon sugar
1/4 teaspoon salt

A touch of sweet chili *sambal* and creamy hollandaise accentuates this combination of finely diced vegetables, fresh herbs, ham, and poached eggs, in this self-indulgent breakfast. Serve with a slice of French bread and, if possible, a balmy tropical breeze for sharpening the appetite. Serve only those vegetables that you have at hand.

1 To prepare the hollandaise, place the egg yolks in a bowl and season with salt and pepper (preferably white pepper). Pour the yolks into a processor and blend thoroughly, about 1 minute. Heat the lemon juice and vinegar until it just begins to simmer, then switch the processor on again and slowly pour the hot lemon mixture into the eggs. Melt the butter (in the same pan as you heated the lemon and vinegar) without burning it and, when it begins to foam, switch on the processor once again and pour the butter into the mixture as slowly as you can. Wipe the bowl and process one last time. Set aside.

2 To prepare the sweet chili *sambal*, heat oil in a small saucepan and add both lots of chilies and garlic. Stir-fry over low-medium heat until fragrant, 4–5 minutes, then add all other ingredients and simmer for 10 minutes. Process to a smooth paste, then return to saucepan and keep warm.

3 To finalize the dish, heat clarified butter in a saucepan. Add onion and stir-fry over moderate heat for 2 minutes. Add ham and cook for 2 minutes. Add all the vegetables and herbs and season with salt and pepper, stirring to mix well and heat the vegetables through.

4 Transfer the ham and vegetables to 4 plates. Top each serving with 2 poached eggs, 2–3 tablespoons of the hollandaise sauce and a dollop of sweet *sambal*. Serve with toasted French bread, and garnish with a sprig of parsley, if desired.

Note: To make hollandaise by hand, simply pour the hot lemon mixture into the eggs while whisking continuously by hand. Repeat with the melted butter. To save time, you could make the sweet *sambal* a day or two in advance and refrigerate it until needed, or use purchased *sambal*. To make poached eggs, use an egg poacher or bring a skillet of water, with a few drops of vinegar added, to simmering point. Carefully crack open the eggs, a few at a time, into the water. Simmer very gently until set, about 2–3 minutes, then remove the eggs with a slotted spoon and repeat with remaining eggs.

Chicken congee with Taiwan-style accompaniments

3 quarts (3 liters) light chicken stock
5 oz (150 g) chicken breast
1/2 cup (100 g) short-grain rice
2 tablespoons very finely sliced scallion
(spring onion)
1 1/2 tablespoons very finely julienned
young ginger
2 tablespoons crsip-fried garlic slices
(see Note), or 1/3 oz (10 g) dried rice
vermicelli, deep-fried until crisp
Liberal sprinkling of white pepper

Condiments
1 century egg, coarsely chopped
1 salted duck egg, coarsely chopped
1 1/2 tablespoons canned salted
cabbage, finely chopped
1 1/2 tablespoons pickled radish
(*tang choy*)
3 tablespoons canned braised peanuts
1 large red chili, thinly sliced
2 tablespoons light soy sauce
2 squares fermented red bean curd,
halved
1/2 cup (60 g) flaked canned dace fish
with preserved black beans

Millions of Chinese around the world start the day with comforting congee or rice porridge, a simple gruel of rice and water eaten with various condiments. The Taiwanese version is more "soupy" than most types, and this recipe has more flavor, thanks to the chicken stock. Taiwanese congee is also distinguishable by the large range of often-salty accompaniments. It is not essential to serve all these, but the more you have, the more delicious the result. This congee is equally good as a light lunch.

1 Put the chicken stock and chicken breast in a large saucepan and bring to a boil. Lower heat, cover, and simmer very gently until the chicken is cooked, about 15 minutes. Remove the chicken, cool, then shred.
2 Add the rice to the pan and bring to a boil, stirring. Partly cover the saucepan and simmer, stirring from time to time, until the rice has broken up and the stock reduced to a thick mixture, about 1 hour. Divide between 4 bowls, then add the shredded chicken, scallion, ginger, crisp-fried garlic, and pepper to each bowl.
3 While the rice is cooking, put as many of the condiments as desired in separate small bowls and serve with the hot congee for adding according to taste.

Note: To make crisp-fried garlic slices, fry sliced garlic in oil over medium heat until golden brown. Do not over-brown. Remove with a slotted spoon and drain on paper towel. Store in a dry, airtight jar to preserve their crispness. Most Asian stores sell cans of braised peanuts, salted cabbage, and dace with preserved black beans, plus jars of red bean curd; pickled radish is generally available in plastic packs.

Black rice pudding

1 1/2 cups (375 g) black glutinous rice,
   washed and drained
1/2 cup (125 g) white glutinous rice,
   washed and drained
3/4 cup (185 ml) thick coconut milk

Syrup
6 cups (1 1/2 liters) water
1/2 cup (125 g) sugar
2 tablespoons chopped palm sugar
1 pandan (screwpine) leaf, raked with
   a fork and tied, or pandan essence
   to taste
1 teaspoon salt

Served with deep-fried bananas with hazelnut filling and a cup of strong black coffee, this black rice pudding is an indulgent way to start the day.

1 Place both lots of rice in a bowl, add hot water to cover and leave to soak, 30 minutes. Drain. Line the rack of a steamer with a damp kitchen cloth. Spread the rice evenly on top and cover the steamer. Place the steamer over a wok of boiling water, adding boiling water every 10 minutes, and steam until the rice has swollen and is slightly soft, about 45 minutes. If liked, the steamed rice could be refrigerated overnight.
2 To make the syrup, put all the ingredients in a large saucepan and bring to a boil, stirring until the sugar dissolves. Add the steamed rice and simmer, stirring from time to time, until the rice is very soft and the mixture has reached a porridge-like consistency, about 1 hour. Add more water if required to stop the rice from becoming too dry. Remove the pandan leaf and serve warm with a jug of thick coconut milk for adding to taste.

Note: An alternative, and slightly easier, method to cook this dish is to omit the steaming altogether and to put the washed and drained rice in a pan with water to cover by about 1 1/4 in (3 cm). The rice is simmered until slightly soft, the syrup added to the pan and cooking continued until the right texture is achieved.

Deep-fried bananas with hazelnut filling

8 finger bananas, or 4 large bananas
Vegetable oil for deep-frying

Hazelnut filling
2 tablespoons finely chopped palm
   sugar (or soft brown sugar)
2 tablespoons water
2/3 cup (70 g) finely ground hazelnut
   meal, toasted in a dry pan
1 tablespoon cocoa powder
Scant 1/2 cup (50 g) confectioners'
   (icing) sugar
1 tablespoon lime or lemon juice

Batter
1 cup (125 g) flour
3 tablespoons cornstarch
2 teaspoons superfine (caster) sugar
1 teaspoon baking powder
Pinch of salt
3/4–1 cup (185–250 ml) water

In this more sophisticated version of Balinese *pisang godoh*—bananas dipped in batter and deep-fried—you fill each banana with a sweet hazelnut-chocolate mixture before dipping it in batter and deep-frying it. You can use either sweet finger bananas or regular large bananas.

1 Prepare hazelnut filling by heating the palm sugar and water in a small saucepan, stirring. Simmer 2 minutes to reduce the volume to 2 tablespoons. Pour into a bowl and stir in all the other ingredients, mixing well. Set aside.
2 To prepare the batter, put all ingredients except water into a bowl, stirring to mix. Make a well in the center and stir in the water to make a thick batter. Set aside.
3 Peel each banana and make a deep lengthways cut in each. Spoon in about 2 teaspoons of the hazelnut mixture and gently squeeze the banana to close.
4 Heat oil in a wok. When very hot, dip each banana in batter to coat well, then carefully add to the oil. Deep-fry until the bananas are golden brown all over, 2–3 minutes. Drain well on paper towel and serve hot.

Note: You could save time by using ready made hazelnut-chocolate paste such as Nutella, mixed with a little lime or lemon juice, to fill each banana.

Masala dosai

1 1/2 cups (300 g) long-grain rice
3/4 cup (150 g) husked black gram
  lentils (*urad* or *ulundoo*), usually sold
  with black skins removed thus pale
  creamy white in color
1 teaspoon salt
Vegetable oil for frying

Potato filling
1 tablespoon turmeric powder
2–3 teaspoons chili powder
2 tablespoons water
2 tablespoons vegetable oil
1 onion, finely chopped
1 teaspoon brown mustard seeds
10–12 curry leaves
4 medium potatoes (1 lb or 500 g),
  boiled and cut in 1/2-in (1-cm) dice
1 teaspoon salt

Dhal
2 tablespoons vegetable oil
1 1/2 teaspoons brown mustard seeds
1 medium onion, thinly sliced
2 cloves garlic, finely chopped
10–12 curry leaves
1 dried chili, cut in 1/2-in (1-cm) lengths
1 1/2 cups (250 g) yellow lentils, soaked
  15 minutes, drained
1 clove garlic, left whole
1 teaspoon salt
4 cups (1 liter) water
1 teaspoon turmeric powder
1 teaspoon chili powder
1 small carrot, diced
1 small potato, diced
1 medium tomato, diced
1 large red chili, sliced, to garnish
  (optional)
1 small onion, cut in rings, to garnish
1 sprig fresh cilantro (coriander) leaves
  to garnish

Tomato chutney
4–6 medium ripe tomatoes
  (1 lb or 500 g), chopped
2 large red chilies, sliced
2 tablespoons vegetable oil
1 medium onion, thinly sliced
1 teaspoon brown mustard seeds
10–12 curry leaves
1 tablespoon coriander powder
Salt and black pepper to taste

Masala dosai—as these delectable southern Indian pancakes are known—are wrapped around a spiced potato filling and accompanied by a yellow lentil *dhal*, fresh tomato chutney, and fresh coconut chutney (see page 184). Prepare some or all of the accompaniments the night before and make the pancakes fresh for breakfast.

1 To prepare the pancakes, soak the rice and black gram lentils overnight in plenty of cold water to cover. Drain and transfer both rice and lentils to a food processor. Process, adding just a little water as needed until the mixture is very smooth. Transfer to a bowl, add salt and stir in sufficient water to make a thin creamy consistency. (The batter can now be kept at room temperature for maximum 4–6 hours before it begins to ferment slightly.)
2 Make the potato filling by mixing turmeric and chili powders with the water to make a paste. Heat the oil in a wok or wide saucepan and add the onion, mustard seeds, and curry leaves. Stir-fry over low–moderate heat, 1 minute, then add the spice paste and stir-fry 2 minutes. Add the diced potatoes and stir to mix and thoroughly coat the potatoes with the spice mixture, 2 minutes. Set aside and prepare the lentil stew and chutneys.
3 Shortly before the pancakes are required, stir the batter and add more water, if needed, to achieve the consistency of a thin cream; the batter must not be too thick. Heat a large non-stick frying pan and grease the bottom with about 1 teaspoon oil. Add about 1/3 cup of batter and quickly tilt the saucepan around to swirl the batter out from the center to the edges of the pan. Cook over high heat until the underneath is golden brown and the top is dry, about 1 1/2 minutes. Turn the pancake over and cook until golden brown under, about 1 minute. Stack on a plate, and continue cooking, adding more oil to the frying pan as needed, until all the batter is used up.
4 Fill each pancake with some of the potato filling, and serve accompanied by *dhal*, tomato chutney, and fresh coconut chutney (see page 184).

Note: To cook pancakes, it is important to have a thin batter, and to cook over high heat. Do not flip the pancake until the top is completely dry.

Dhal
Heat oil in a saucepan and add mustard seeds, onion, garlic, curry leaves, and dried chili. Stir-fry over medium heat, 3 minutes. Add drained lentils, whole garlic clove, salt, and water. Bring to a boil, simmer until starting to soften, about 15 minutes. Mix the turmeric and chili powders with 2 tablespoons water to form a paste, then add to the lentils together with the carrot, potato and tomato. Simmer until vegetables are soft, 15–20 minutes. Garnish with onion rings and cilantro.

Tomato chutney
Process tomatoes and chilies until finely ground. Heat the oil in a saucepan and stir-fry the onion, mustard seeds, curry leaves, and coriander powder over low–moderate heat, 2–3 minutes. Add the processed mixture, stirring well. Bring to a boil, lower heat, and simmer uncovered for 10 minutes. Add salt and pepper to taste.

Assorted lassi

Sweet *lassi*
2 cups (500 ml) chilled plain yogurt
1 cup (250 ml) chilled milk (or water)
2–3 tablespoons sugar
8–12 ice cubes

Salted *lassi*
2 cups (500 ml) chilled plain yogurt
1 1/2 cups (375 ml) iced water
1/2–1 teaspoon salt
4 ice cubes
1/4–1/2 teaspoon *chaat masala* or
 ground cumin, optional

Spicy *lassi*
2 1/2 cups (625 ml) chilled plain yogurt
1/2 teaspoon salt
2 large green chilies, chopped
1/2 cup (125 ml) iced water
4–8 ice cubes

Masala *lassi*
2 1/2 cups (625 ml) chilled plain yogurt
1/2 teaspoon salt
2 tablespoons chopped fresh cilantro
 (coriander) leaves
10–12 fresh curry leaves, chopped
1 tablespoon very finely chopped fresh
 ginger
2 tablespoons very finely chopped
 onion
8–12 ice cubes
1/4 teaspoon cumin powder

Rose-flavored *lassi* with pistachios
3 cups (750 ml) plain yogurt, chilled
3 tablespoons sugar
2 teaspoons rose water, or few drops
 rose essence
6–8 ice cubes
2 teaspoons finely crushed raw
 pistachio nuts

Papaya *lassi*
2 cups (500 ml) chilled skim milk
3/4 cup (185 ml) chilled plain yogurt
10 oz (300 g) ripe papaya, diced
1 1/2 teaspoons lime juice
4 tablespoons honey
4 ice cubes

Known in India as *lassi*, these deliciously refreshing iced yogurt drinks may be drunk sweetened with sugar, lightly salted, or flavored with virtually any fruits and spices of your choice. Our spicy *lassi* is blended with green chili, our *masala lassi* is flavored with a little onion, fresh ginger, curry leaves, and fresh cilantro, and our rose-flavored *lassi* with pistachios is an elegant combination that pleases both palate and eye. Use homemade yogurt whenever possible (see Note).

Sweet *lassi*
Put all ingredients in a blender and process until smooth. Serve, or chill longer if desired.

Salted *lassi*
Put yogurt, water, salt, and ice cubes in a blender and process until smooth. Serve with a pinch of spice on top if desired.

Spicy *lassi*
Put 1/2 cup (125 ml) of the yogurt, salt, and chilies in a blender and process until smooth, adding a little more yogurt if necessary to keep the mixture turning. Pour through a fine sieve, pressing down gently with the back of a spoon. Discard any residue. Return the yogurt mixture to the blender, add the remaining yogurt, water, and ice cubes and process for a few seconds. Divide between 4 glasses. Garnish with a few slices of chili if desired.

Masala *lassi*
Put 1/2 cup (125 ml) of the yogurt, salt, cilantro and curry leaves, ginger, and onion in a blender and process until smooth, adding a little more yogurt if necessary to keep the mixture turning. Pour through a fine sieve, pressing down gently with the back of a spoon. Discard any residue. Return the yogurt mixture to the blender, add the remaining yogurt and ice cubes and process for a few seconds. Divide between 4 glasses, and sprinkle the top of each serving with a little cumin powder. Serve immediately.

Rose-flavored *lassi* with pistachios
Process yogurt, sugar, rose water, and ice cubes in a blender until smooth. Transfer to 4 chilled glasses and sprinkle the top of each with 1/2 teaspoon crushed pistachio.

Papaya *lassi*
Combine all ingredients in a blender and process at high speed until smooth. Pour into 4 glasses and serve immediately.

Note: To make homemade yogurt, slowly heat 4 cups (1 liter) milk until bubbles start to appear around the edge of the pan—do not let it boil. (For a rich yogurt use 1 cup cream to 3 cups milk, or add 2 heaped tablespoons full cream milk powder to 4 cups milk.) Turn off heat and let milk stand about 15 minutes until you can immerse a finger for just 10 seconds without it stinging. Put 1 tablespoon commercial natural yogurt into a jar. Add the warm milk, stirring constantly. Cover with a towel and keep in a warm place (such as an airing cupboard or warm oven) until the yogurt sets, about 4–6 hours. Use some of this batch as the starter to make your next lot of yogurt.

tropical noon

You've spent the morning exploring the local market, snorkeling over a reef, hiking up the side of a volcano, or simply lazing around the pool with a book. You've got a ravenous appetite but, with the warmth of the midday sun, you want something light. Browse through these recipes and you'll find plenty to inspire you.   Soups range from a Chinese sweet corn and leek soup with crab and coriander dumplings, to carrot and lime leaf broth with shrimps and asparagus, or the unusual dish of seafood and spinach broth with glutinous cheese dumplings.   Fresh, spicy salads make superb appetizers, or light lunches in themsleves — try a salad of raw fish "cooked" in a lime, soy, and sesame dressing, or a heartier spicy, roasted, and herbed Balinese chicken salad. Vegetarian dishes abound with such offerings as tempura tofu with sweet and sour sesame garlic sauce, or fragrant vegetables in spicy laksa broth.   Noodles are a great standby throughout Asia and, when it comes to fried noodles, the Thais are famed for their fried rice-flour noodles, stir-fried with loads of garlic, eggs, bean sprouts, and seasonings; our vegetarian version adds extra vegetables. Other noodle dishes include stir-fried noodles with bean sprouts and chives, Indonesian fried noodles with prawns, vegetables, and sweet soy sauce, and Jakarta-style noodles in chicken stock with delightful deep-fried chicken dumplings. And don't forget *laksa*, the ultimate noodle soup with spicy coconut milk.   If you like fish, you can choose between Maldivian fish curry with fresh pineapple, pan-fried fish fillet with mango, steamed fish in lemongrass, or what about wok-fried clams with Chinese seasonings?   You've earned a little self indulgence, so why not try one of the divine desserts? There's coconut, palm honey, and pandan ice cream, soy milk pannacotta with tropical fruits, and the ultimate in cheese cakes: passion fruit-topped refrigerator cheese cake.

Sweet corn and leek soup with crab and coriander dumplings

1/4 cup (60 g) unsalted butter
1 large onion, chopped
4–5 cloves garlic, finely chopped
1/2 stalk celery, chopped
8 oz (250 g) white portion of leek, thinly
 sliced
2 cups (250 g) fresh or defrosted sweet
 corn kernels
1 bay leaf
4 cups (1 liter) chicken stock
Salt and pepper to taste
1 small tomato, cut in small cubes, to
 garnish
1 scallion (spring onion), finely
 chopped, to garnish
Bread sticks to garnish

Crab and coriander dumplings
1 cup (125 g) cooked crabmeat, picked
 over for any cartilage
1/2 cup (75 g) minced chicken
1 clove garlic, finely chopped
1 tablespoon finely chopped fresh
 cilantro (coriander) leaves
1/4 teaspoon coriander powder
3 tablespoons heavy (thick) cream
1/4 teaspoon salt
Liberal sprinkling white pepper
16 fresh or defrosted *won ton* wrappers
2 teaspoons cornstarch

This elegant, creamy soup is made with leek, sweet corn, celery, and chicken stock, and is served with tiny dumplings of crabmeat mixed with chicken and perfumed with fresh and dried coriander. With its subtle yet satisfying flavors, it makes a perfect start to any meal.

1 Heat butter in a large saucepan, then stir-fry onion and garlic over low–moderate heat until transparent, about 3 minutes. Add celery, leek, and sweet corn and stir-fry until softened, about 4 minutes. Add bay leaf and stock and bring to a boil. Cover, lower heat, and simmer until the vegetables are soft, 20–25 minutes. Cool while preparing the dumplings.
2 To prepare the dumplings, combine crabmeat, chicken, garlic, fresh cilantro leaves, coriander powder, cream, salt, and pepper in a food processor, and pulse several times to mix well. Moisten the edges of a *won ton* wrapper with a finger dipped in water, then put 1 heaped teaspoon of the crabmeat mixture in the center. Lift up the sides and pinch together in the center to seal. Sprinkle a plate with cornstarch and put the filled dumpling on top. Repeat with remaining filling and wrappers. Set aside.
3 Blend or process the soup until smooth. Push through a fine strainer and season to taste with salt and pepper. Reheat soup slowly, then keep warm while cooking the dumplings.
4 Bring a large pan of water to a boil. Add the dumplings, a few at a time, and simmer gently until they rise to the surface and are cooked, about 3 minutes. Drain.
5 Divide the soup between four bowls, and add four dumplings to each serving. Garnish with tomato, scallion, and bread sticks. Serve hot.

Seafood and spinach soup with glutinous cheese dumplings

2 1/2 tablespoons margerine
1 1/2 tablespoons all-purpose (plain) flour
4 raw medium shrimps, peeled and deveined
4 fresh scallops
1 heaped cup (75 g) spinach leaves, finely chopped
4 cups (1 liter) chicken stock
1 1/2 teaspoons Chinese rice wine
Small pinch of salt and white pepper
4 tablespoons whipping cream (optional)

Glutinous cheese dumplings
1/2 cup (60 g) glutinous rice flour
1 tablespoon vegetable shortening
3 tablespoons water (or more as required)
8 balls of mature cheddar cheese, about 3/4-in (1 1/2-cm) in diameter

This unusual soup has as its basis a chicken stock made creamy with a flour and margarine roux. Cooked shrimps, scallops, and spinach are added to the soup, which is served with dumplings made from glutinous rice flour dough wrapped around a ball of cheese. Add a little cream to finish the soup if you're in a self-indulgent mood.

1 To make the dumplings, sift flour into a bowl and add the shortening. Make a well in the center and slowly add the water, a little at a time, stirring with a wooden spoon and finishing off using your hands to form a soft, plaible, moist dough that leaves the side of the bowl (and your fingers) clean.
2 Roll the dough into a sausage and divide into 8 portions. Roll each portion into a ball, hold in the palm of one hand and press with your fingers to flatten into a disc, about 2 in (5 cm) in diameter. Place a cheese ball in the center of each disc and fold the dough around the cheese ball to enclose it. When ready to cook, bring a large pan of water to the boil and add dumplings. Simmer until dumplings rise to the surface and are cooked, about 6–8 minutes.
3 Melt the margerine and whisk in the flour to make a smooth roux. Set aside.
4 Blanch the shrimps and scallops, drain and set aside. Blanch the chopped spinach, drain and set aside.
5 Heat the chicken stock in a wok or pan and add Chinese rice wine, salt, and pepper. Add the seafood and spinach, then stir in the roux. Finally add the cream to taste. Divide between four bowls and add two dumplings to each bowl.

Chinese Executive Chef Jereme Leung—Singapore

Carrot and kaffir lime leaf broth with shrimps and asparagus

375 ml (1 1/2 cups) fresh carrot juice
16 medium raw shrimps, peeled and deveined, final tail section left intact
4 stems lemongrass, very finely chopped
1–2 large red chilies, finely chopped
1 tablespoon finely chopped fresh cilantro (coriander) leaves
1 tablespoon finely chopped fresh mint
4 kaffir lime leaves, very finely shredded lengthways
4 very small baby carrots, blanched
4 very small baby turnips, blanched
8 fresh green asparagus spears, sliced and blanched
4 very small baby zucchini (courgettes), blanched, or 1 1/3 oz (40 g) zucchini (courgettes), sliced and blanched
2 tablespoons fish sauce, or more to taste
1 tablespoon lime juice, or more to taste
Salt and freshly ground black pepper to taste
2/3 cup (120 g) unsalted butter, diced
Sprigs of fresh cilantro (coriander) leaves to garnish

This inspired combination of tropical Asian flavors — lemongrass, cilantro, chilies, fish sauce, and lime juice — with shrimps, fresh carrot juice, and baby vegetables is not only full of flavor and nutrition, but is so attractive that it can be served on any occasion. The cooking broth is enriched with butter, French-style, making this a sophisticated example of East meeting West.

1 Put the carrot juice in a saucepan and add the shrimps, lemongrass, chilies, cilantro, mint, and lime leaves. Bring to a boil, stirring once or twice, then add the vegetables and simmer just until the shrimps are cooked, about 3 minutes.
2 Season to taste with fish sauce, lime juice, salt, and pepper. Remove the shrimps and vegetables with a slotted spoon and place in a bowl. Add the butter to the liquid in the pan and cook over low heat, whisking constantly, until the butter is absorbed. Pour over the shrimps and vegetables, garnish with cilantro and serve immediately.

Sailing on the Indian Ocean—Four Seasons Resort Maldives

Raw fish salad with soy, lime, and sesame dressing

10 oz (300 g) skinned and boneless dorab or wolf herring fillet (see Note)
5 oz (150 g) long white radish (daikon), julienned
10 oz (300 g) Japanese cucumber, julienned (substitute with small Western cucumber, seeds removed)
1 large red chili, seeded and finely shredded lengthways
3/4 in (2 cm) ginger, thinly sliced
4 sprigs fresh cilantro (coriander) leaves and stems
1 tablespoon chopped scallion (spring onion)
4 baby pickled onions (optional)
2 teaspoons sesame seeds, toasted until golden brown
1 tablespoon finely chopped chervil or parsely
2 tablespoons salmon roe, optional

Dressing
2 tablespoons lime or lemon juice
1 tablespoon light soy sauce
2 teaspoons peanut oil, or shallot oil (see below)
2 teaspoons sesame oil
2 teaspoons Chinese rice wine, preferably Shao Hsing
2 teaspoons sugar
1/2 teaspoon salt
Liberal sprinkling white pepper

Shallot oil
1 oz (30 g) shallots, peeled, halved
1 oz (30 g) large onions, peeled, halved
1 oz (30 g) ginger, peeled, halved
1 oz (30 g) garlic, peeled, smashed
2 1/2 cups (600 ml) vegetable (not olive) oil

Dishes where fresh fish is "cooked" with a dressing or marinade of lime juice are common throughout tropical Asia. Chinese from the southern province of Guangdong enjoy raw fish salad during the annual Lunar New Year celebrations, and their classic recipe has inspired this modern interpretation. Tangy, fragrant, and with contrasting textures, this makes an ideal starter or light lunch.

1 Chill the fish in the freezer for 10–15 minutes to firm. Cut into very thin slices, about 2 x 1 in (5 x 2 cm).
2 While fish is chilling, blanch the julienned radish in boiling water for 1 minute. Drain well, then transfer to a bowl of iced water to cool. Drain again and squeeze lightly to expel all moisture.
3 Prepare the dressing by combining and whisking all ingredients together in a small bowl. If you are using shallot oil, make a large batch of homemade oil. Combine shallots, onions, ginger, garlic, and oil in a large pan and cook over medium heat until most of the ingredients are golden brown and fragrant. Leave to cool, then pass through a sieve and pour the oil into a bottle.
4 Arrange radish, cucumber, chili, ginger, and coriander on a serving plate, then top with slices of fish, and sprinkle with scallion and sesame seeds. Garnish with salmon roe, if using. Drizzle with dressing just before serving. Serve immediately.

Note: Wolf herring can be replaced with baby barracuda or fine-fleshed white fish such as Spanish mackerel or pomfret.

Tuna cakes with banana chutney and green curry dip

1 cup (125 g) flour
Pinch of salt
1/3 cup (85 ml) water
1 tablespoon vegetable oil

Tuna filling
2/3 cup (100 g) firmly packed drained
  cannned tuna
2 tablespoons very finely chopped
  onion
2 tablespoons very finely chopped fresh
  cilantro (coriander) leaves
2 tablespoons freshly grated or
  moistened desiccated coconut
2 teaspoons lime juice
Salt to taste

Banana chutney
2 teaspoons vegetable oil
1 teaspoon mustard seeds
10 curry leaves
2 dried red chilies, soaked in water
  5 minutes, roughly chopped
2 medium ripe but firm banana, roughly
  mashed
6 tablespoons orange juice
1 teaspoon turmeric powder (optional)
Salt and black pepper to taste

Green curry dip
4 teaspoons finely chopped ginger
4 teaspoons finely chopped garlic
1 large green chili, chopped
1 cup (40 g) coarsely chopped fresh
  cilantro (coriander) leaves and fine
  stems
1 cup (40 g) coarsely chopped fresh
  mint leaves
2 tablespoons coconut or vegetable oil
1 teaspoon brown mustard seeds
1 teaspoon cumin seeds
1 large onion, chopped
10 curry leaves
1 large tomato, peeled and chopped
2 teaspoons curry powder
3/4 cup (185 ml) coconut milk
1/2 teaspoon salt

Most fish cakes combine flaked fish with mashed potato, but this unusual version encases a lightly seasoned mixture of canned tuna in a simple homemade pastry. The flavor of the tuna cakes is enhanced by a coconut sauce rich in fresh herbs, and an easily made fresh banana chutney.

1 Prepare the tuna filling by combining all ingredients in a bowl, mixing well. Set aside.
2 Combine flour, salt, and water in a bowl. Knead for 5 minutes to make a pliable dough. Divide into 8 balls, then flatten each with the palm of your hand. Press with the thumbs and fingers to make each ball into a circle about 3 1/4 in (8 cm) in diameter. Fill each circle with one-eighth of the tuna, then lift up the sides, pleating and squeezing them to the center to enclose the filling. Flatten gently into a cake about 2 in (5 cm) in diameter, then heat 1 tablespoon oil in a large skillet and sear the tuna cakes until golden brown, about 1 1/2 minutes on each side. Transfer tuna cakes to a baking tray and bake in an oven at 350°F (180°C, gas 4) for 8 minutes.
3 To prepare the banana chutney, heat oil in a small pan and add mustard seeds, curry leaves, and dried chilies. Stir-fry until the seeds crackle, then add the banana and mix well with a wooden spoon, cooking for 1 minute. Stir in the orange juice and turmeric, and season with salt and pepper, then transfer to a bowl. Cool, then chill in the refrigerator.
4 For the green curry dip, process ginger, garlic, chili, cilantro, and mint leaves together to make a smooth paste. Heat the oil in a pan and add mustard and cumin seeds. Stir-fry over medium heat until they crackle, then add onion and curry leaves. Stir-fry until the onion softens, 3–4 minutes, then add tomato and cook 5 minutes.
5 Add the blended paste and cook, stirring frequently, 4–5 minutes. Pour in coconut milk, add salt and bring slowly to a boil, stirring. Simmer uncovered until the sauce thickens, about 8 minutes. Taste and add more salt if desired.
6 Serve the tuna cakes with banana chutney and green curry dip.

Note: If desired, garnish the cakes with fried curry leaves and chili.

Shredded spiced chicken salad

1 fresh chicken, about 3 lb (1 1/2 kg), halved, skin discarded
1 stem lemongrass, sliced
4 cloves garlic, chopped
1 teaspoon salt
1/4 teaspoon freshly ground black pepper
2 tablespoons vegetable oil
6 oz (180 g) long beans, sliced diagonally in 1 1/2-in (4-cm) lengths, boiled until cooked but still firm, drained
1 tablespoon lime juice
2–3 large red chilies, seeded and finely chopped
3 kaffir lime leaves, finely shredded
1/2 cup (20 g) firmly packed lemon basil leaves, washed and dried
Lime halves, for adding to taste

Dried shrimp paste *sambal*
3 tablespoons vegetable oil
5 shallots, finely chopped
2 cloves garlic, finely chopped
6–8 large red chilies, finely chopped
1 tablespoon dried shrimp paste, roasted
1 small tomato, finely chopped
1 1/2 tablespoons sugar
1/2 teaspoon salt
1/4 teaspoon freshly ground black pepper

This Balinese classic begins with chicken seasoned with salt, garlic, and lemongrass. After roasting, the meat is shredded and mixed with beans, chilies, kaffir lime leaves, lime juice, lemon basil, and dried shrimp paste *sambal* to make a tangy, fragrant treat. Both the chicken and the dressing can be prepared in advance, and combined at the last minute.

1 Preheat oven to 350°F (180°C, gas 4).
2 Prick the chicken all over with a fork to allow the marinade to penetrate. Process the lemongrass, garlic, salt, and pepper in a spice grinder, adding just a little of the oil to make a smooth paste. Transfer the mixture to a bowl and stir in the remaining oil. Coat the chicken all over with the paste, place on a baking dish and set on a rack in the preheated oven and cook for 45 minutes. Allow to cool and shred the flesh by hand. Set aside.
3 While the chicken is cooking, make the dried shrimp paste *sambal*. Heat oil in a small pan and add the shallots, garlic, chilies, shrimp paste, and tomato. Stir-fry over low-medium heat until fragrant, 3–4 minutes. Add sugar, salt, and pepper and cook 10 minutes, stirring frequently to prevent the mixture from sticking. Cool and blend coarsely before using.
4 Just before the salad is required, put the chicken in a large bowl and add the shrimp paste *sambal*. Toss to mix well then add the long beans, lime juice, chilies, lime leaves, and basil. Toss again. Taste and add salt and freshly ground black pepper if desired. Serve at room temperature with a lime half for adding lime juice to taste.

Note: Be sure to shred the chicken by hand rather than with a knife for the best result. Do not overcook the beans; when they are still firm, drain and plunge in ice-cold water, then drain again.

Mesmerizing Balinese dance—Jimbaran Bay

Tempura tofu with sweet and sour sesame garlic sauce

1 lb (500 g) silken Japanese tofu, cut in 1 1/4-in (3-cm) cubes (see Note)
12 asparagus spears, thick stalks trimmed
3/4 cup (100 g) tempura flour (see Note)
1/3 cup (90 ml) iced water
Vegetable oil for deep frying
2 cups (125 g) young spinach leaves, washed and drained
4 sprigs fresh basil, leaves torn
1 tablespoon crisp-fried garlic slices
2–3 dried salt fish, or anchovies

Sauce
1/2 cup (125 ml) bottled Thai sweet chili sauce
1/4 cup (60 ml) fish sauce
1/4 cup (60 ml) rice vinegar
2 teaspoons sesame oil
2 cloves garlic, finely minced
1 scallion (spring onion), finely chopped

1 Lay the tofu pieces on kitchen towel and leave to drain thoroughly.
2 Prepare the sauce by combining all the ingredients in a small bowl and mixing well.
3 Broil, grill, or steam the asparagus spears until just cooked, about 5 minutes.
4 Put tempura flour in a bowl and stir in the iced water, mixing with a pair of chopsticks. Do not over-mix; several small lumps are normal in tempura batter.
5 Put oil in a wok and heat until very hot. Dip several piece of tofu in the batter, using two wooden spoons to turn and coat well. Transfer tofu, one piece at a time, to the oil. Cook, turning to brown on all sides. Drain on paper towel and repeat with remaining tofu and batter.
6 Divide the spinach, basil, and asparagus between 4 serving plates, and add tofu to each. Spoon over the sauce and garnish each dish with crisp-fried garlic.

Note: If using rolls of silken tofu, cut across in 1 1/4-in (3-cm) slices. If tempura flour (which gives the batter a very crisp light texture) is not available, replace it with 3/4 cup (100 g) sifted all-purpose (plain) flour and 1 egg yolk.

Hokkien noodles

3 tablespoons vegetable oil
4 eggs, lightly beaten
4 cloves garlic, finely chopped
1 lb 3 oz (600 g) fresh yellow (Hokkien) noodles
6 1/2 oz (200 g) fresh rice-flour (laksa) noodles
1 1/2 cups (150 g) bean sprouts
5 oz (150 g) fish cake, sliced (optional)
16–20 cooked small shrimps, peeled and deveined
5 oz (150 g) cooked squid, sliced
5 oz (150 g) cooked pork, sliced
1/2 cup (60 g) chopped garlic chives (*kuchye*), in 1 1/4-in (3-cm) lengths
Salt and white pepper to taste
2 medium red chilies, sliced, to garnish
4 round green small limes (kalamansi or *limau kesturi*), or 1 large lime, quartered, to garnish

Pork stock
2 lb (1 kg) chicken carcass for stock, blanched in boiling water 3 minutes
2 lb (1 kg) pork bones, blanched in boiling water 3 minutes
6 cups (1 1/2 liters) water
3 in (8 cm) fresh ginger, bruised
3 whole cloves garlic, bruised
1 1/2 teaspoons salt

Sambal belacan
8–10 large red chilies, chopped
10 shallots, chopped
1 tablespoon dried shrimp paste, toasted
2 tablespoons lime juice
1 teaspoon sugar
1 teaspoon salt
4 round green small limes (kalamansi or *limau kesturi*), top sliced off, or 1 large lime, quartered

Hokkien *mee* (noodles), as this dish is known in Singapore, originated in southern China, in Fujian province. A mixture of yellow noodles and rice-flour noodles is stir-fried with eggs, bean sprouts, chives, seafood, and pork, then simmered in pork stock. A distinctly local touch comes in the accompanying *sambal belacan*, a pungent paste of chilies, shallots, dried shrimp paste, and lime. This hearty noodle dish can be enjoyed any time of the day or night.

1 To prepare the pork stock, put the blanched carcasses and bones in a pan with the water, ginger, and garlic. Bring to a boil, cover, reduce heat and simmer 2 hours. Strain, discarding bones, then boil the stock with the pan uncovered if necessary to reduce the stock to 2 cups (500 ml). Set aside.
2 Make the *sambal belacan* by processing all ingredients except the limes in a blender until finely ground. Transfer to 4 small sauce dishes, add a lime to each and set aside.
3 Just before the noodles are required, heat half of the oil in a large wok until very hot. Add the egg and stir-fry until it just starts to set, then add remaining oil and the garlic and stir-fry 10 seconds. Add both lots of noodles, bean sprouts, fish cake, shrimps, squid, and pork and stir-fry for 1–2 minutes, using two wok spatulas to mix the ingredients thoroughly.
4 Add 2 cups (500 ml) prepared pork stock and stir until the liquid is almost dried up. Season with salt and pepper and transfer to a serving dish. Scatter with the garlic chives and serve accompanied by the *sambal*, sliced chilies, and lime.

Note: If you do not have a very large wok, you may need to cook the noodles in two separate batches. If you cannot obtain fresh rice-flour noodles, use 3 1/2 oz (100 g) dried rice vermicelli, soaked in warm water to soften it.

Mi goreng

2 tablespoons sesame oil
2 tablespoons oyster sauce
4 teaspoons fish sauce
4 teaspoons sweet soy sauce
4 teaspoons chili sauce
4 teaspoons Chinese rice wine
1/4 cup (60 ml) vegetable oil
6–8 cloves garlic, chopped
13 oz (400 g) raw shrimps, peeled and
   deveined, halved lengthways
1 medium onion, thinly sliced
1/2 medium carrot, finely julienned
4 scallions (spring onions), julienned
2 cups (100 g) chopped *choy sum*
   (Chinese flowering cabbage)
2 tablespoons julienned moist pickled
   Chinese cabbage (optional)
2–3 large red chilies, seeded and
   shredded
13 oz (400 g) fresh egg noodles,
   blanched in boiling water, drained
2 eggs, beaten and cooked to make
   a thin omelet, shredded (see Note)
2 tablespoons deep-fried shallots

Noodles are a favorite snack or light meal throughout the region, with literally hundreds of different versions. This Indonesian-style dish of stir-fried egg noodles, known as *mi goreng* in Indonesia, is tasty and easily prepared, containing a mixture of shrimps, leafy greens, garlic, onions, carrot, and chili, plus plenty of seasoning sauces.

1 Combine sesame oil, oyster sauce, fish sauce, soy sauce, chili sauce, and wine in a small bowl and set aside.
2 Heat the oil in a wok and add garlic. Stir-fry for a few seconds, then add the shrimps and stir-fry over very high heat until they start to change color, about 30 seconds. Add the onion, carrot, scallions, both lots of cabbage, and chilies and stir-fry 2 minutes. Pour in the combined sauces, stirring to mix well. Add the noodles, tossing to mix well and heat through, about 1 minute. Transfer to a serving bowl and garnish with omelet and deep-fried shallots.

Note: Make a very thin omelet, roll it up, and slice thinly.

Freshly picked herbs—Four Seasons Resort Jimbaran Bay

Vegetarian fried rice-flour noodles

1 lb 3 oz (600 g) fresh rice-flour
    noodles, or 10 oz (300 g) dried rice
    stick noodles
3 tablespoons vegetable oil
3 sprigs fresh sweet basil leaves
6–8 cloves garlic, very finely chopped
4 eggs, lightly beaten
2 cups (125 g) loosely packed bean
    sprouts, washed and drained, straggly
    tails removed
1 small onion, halved lengthways, thinly
    sliced across
1/2 small carrot, finely julienned
4 large fresh *shiitake* or button
    mushrooms, stems discarded, caps
    shredded
2–3 long beans, cut in 3/4-in (1 1/2-cm)
    lengths
2–3 large red chilies, finely julienned
2–3 bird's-eye chilies, finely chopped
1 scallion (spring onion), cut in 2-in
    (5-cm) lengths, julienned
1 tablespoon paprika
2 tablespoons sugar
1/3 cup (85 ml) fish sauce
1/3 cup (85 ml) lime juice
3 tablespoons coarsely chopped dry
    roasted peanuts
Sprigs of fresh cilantro (coriander)
    leaves to garnish
1 lime or lemon, quartered

This meatless version of fried rice noodles has a light, refreshing flavor. Bean sprouts, carrot, meaty flavored fresh *shiitake* mushrooms and long beans are cooked with garlic, onion, and chilies, with fish sauce (or light soy sauce, if you want to be strictly vegetarian), lime juice, and chopped peanuts adding extra flavor and texture.

1 Cook the noodles in boiling water until *al dente*. Drain in a colander, rinse under cold running water, and drain again. Spread on a large plate.
2 Heat oil in a wok and add the basil leaves. Fry quickly, then remove leaves with a slotted spoon, drain on paper towel and set aside. Add the garlic and stir-fry over medium heat for a few seconds, then add the eggs and stir until they begin to set. Push eggs to the sides, then add the bean sprouts, onion, carrot, mushrooms, long beans, chilies, and scallion and stir-fry until the vegetables are almost cooked, about 2 minutes.
3 Add the noodles, paprika, sugar, fish sauce, and lime juice and stir-fry to mix the noodles thoroughly with the other ingredients and heat through. Transfer to a serving dish and garnish with fried basil leaves, cilantro, peanuts, and lime wedges.

Kuzukiri noodles with piquant sauce and seafood

1/4 cup (60 ml) vegetable oil
1 1/3 oz (40 g) dried scallops (conpoy), soaked in warm water until soft, water reserved, scallop finely shredded and dried with paper towel
1 lb (450 g) *kuzukiri* noodles or 8 oz (250 g) mung bean-thread ("glass" or "transparent") noodles (see Note)
3 1/2 oz (100 g) fresh scallops, cooked 1 1/2–2 minutes in boiling water
3 1/2 oz (100 g) peeled raw shrimps, cooked 2–3 minutes in boiling water
3 1/2 oz (100 g) cooked crabmeat, flaked

Sauce
1 1/2 cups (375 ml) chicken stock
2 tablespoons Chinese black vinegar
2 tablespoons white vinegar
4 teaspoons Japanese soy sauce
3 tablespoons sugar
2 tablespoons finely chopped fresh cilantro (coriander) stems and leaves
1 1/2 teaspoons very finely chopped ginger
4 cloves garlic, very finely chopped
2 shallots, very finely chopped
1 large red chili, very finely chopped
4 tablespoons very finely chopped scallion (spring onion)
1/2 teaspoon sesame oil
Salt to taste

This light, piquant noodle dish combines Japanese *kuzukiri* noodles with seafood and a sauce with a marvellous mixture of two types of vinegar, soy sauce, cilantro leaves, garlic, and a touch of chili. A mixture of fresh seafood is served on top of the noodles, and garnished with crisp-fried shavings of dried scallops, one of the most precious Chinese gourmet foods. The combination works wonderfully, even with substitutes.

1 To prepare the sauce, measure the water reserved from soaking the dried scallops and add sufficient chicken stock to make 1 2/3 cups (420 ml) liquid. Put into a small saucepan and add all other sauce ingredients except salt. Bring to a boil, stirring several times. Lower heat and simmer very gently, with the pan uncovered, for 5 minutes. Taste and add salt if desired. Keep warm.
2 Heat oil in a wok and deep-fry the shredded scallop until crisp and golden brown. Drain on paper towel and keep aside.
3 Bring a large pan of water to a boil, add the *kuzukiri* noodles and boil until soft, about 5 minutes. Drain, then put into cold water to stop cooking. Drain again in a sieve, then pour boiling water over the noodles to reheat. Drain and divide noodles between 4 serving bowls.
4 Place the seafood on top of the noodles, pour over the hot sauce and garnish with the deep-fried scallop. Serve immediately.

Note: If using bean-thread noodles, soak in hot water for 10 minutes, drain in a sieve, then pour over boiling water to reheat. Drain again, then divide between the serving bowls. If preferred, you could use only one type of seafood as a garnish.

Miso and vegetable capellini

5 tablespoons (100 g) yellow *miso* paste plus 2 1/2 tablespoons (50 g) red *miso* paste (see Note)
4 cups (1 liter) *dashi* stock (made with instant *dashi* granules)
1 1/2 tablespoons vegetable oil
1 clove garlic, finely chopped
3 1/2 oz (100 g) broccoli, cut into tiny florets
3/4 cup (50 g) finely julienned leek
4 small fresh *shiitake* or brown mushrooms
2 tablespoons dried *wakame* seaweed, soaked in water 1 minute only, drained
8 oz (250 g) dried *capellini* or other very fine wheat pasta such as angel hair pasta, vermicelli, or *spaghettini*, boiled until *al dente*, drained
4 teaspoons crisp-fried shallots

Increasingly popular around the world, Japanese flavors are also enjoyed in much of Asia. The robust taste of fermented soybean paste (*miso*) is the basis of this recipe where a mixture of stir-fried vegetables and fine pasta is added to *dashi* stock with *miso* for a healthy and very tasty light meal.

1 Put both lots of *miso* in a saucepan and stir in the *dashi* stock. Bring to a boil, then cover and keep warm.
2 Heat oil in a wok and add garlic. Stir-fry for a few seconds until it starts to smell fragrant, then add the broccoli, leek, and mushrooms. Stir-fry over high heat, 2 minutes, then transfer to the hot stock and add the seaweed. Divide the pasta between 4 large bowls and top each with the vegetables and stock. Garnish each portion with 1 teaspoon crisp-fried shallots.

Note: Yellow *miso* is lighter in flavor and slightly less salty than red *miso*; if you cannot find both varieties, use 7 1/2 tablespoons yellow *miso* or 5 tablespoons red *miso*.

Dried wakame seaweed soaked in water

Mushroom and chicken noodle soup with crisp-fried dumplings

13 oz (400 g) fine fresh egg noodles,
  or 6 1/2 oz (200 g) dried noodles,
  cooked, rinsed, and drained
1 1/2 tablespoons oyster sauce
1 1/2 tablespoons sesame oil
2 1/2 cups (125 g) Chinese flowering
  cabbage (*choy sum*), blanched in
  chicken stock
4 dried black mushrooms, soaked to
  soften, cooked in chicken stock,
  shredded
1 cup (80 g) straw mushrooms, sliced
6 1/2 oz (200 g) cooked chicken,
  shredded
4 cups (1 liter) chicken stock
1 tablespoon finely chopped pickled
  white radish (*tong choy*), optional
2 tablespoons finely chopped scallions
  (spring onions)
4 teaspoons deep-fried shallots

Crisp-fried dumplings
2/3 cup (100 g) finely minced chicken
1 clove garlic, very finely chopped
1 1/2 teaspoons Chinese rice wine
1 1/2 teaspoons oyster sauce
Pinch of salt
Liberal sprinkling of white pepper
8 fresh or defrosted large *pangsit*
  wrappers, or *wonton* skins
1 egg yolk, stirred to mix
Vegetable oil for deep-frying

Chili sauce
5 medium red chilies, chopped
2 cloves garlic, chopped
2 tablespoons white vinegar
6 tablespoons water
2 tablespoons sugar
1/2 teaspoon salt, or to taste

Vendors pushing carts along the streets of Jakarta and other Indonesian towns, stopping to sell bowls of noodle soup, were once a common sight. Even though some of the mobile vendors are disappearing, really good noodle soups such as this—flavored with chicken, mushrooms, and vegetable and served with crisp-fried chicken dumplings—can still be enjoyed at home.

1 To prepare the crisp-fried dumplings, combine chicken, garlic, rice wine, oyster sauce, salt, and pepper in a bowl, stirring to mix well. Place *pangsit* wrappers or *wonton* skins on a worktop and brush the edges with egg yolk. Put some of the filling in one corner, then fold over the wrapper to enclose the filling and make a triangle, pressing firmly to seal. Set aside while assembling remainder of recipe.
2 For the chili sauce, blend all of the ingredients until smooth. Taste and add more sugar or salt if necessary.
3 To prepare the noodles, put hot drained noodles in a bowl and toss with oyster sauce and sesame oil. Divide noodles between 4 bowls and add some of the cabbage, mushroom, and chicken. Bring the stock to the boil and keep hot.
4 Heat oil in a wok until very hot but not smoking. Add the dumplings and deep-fry in hot oil until crisp and golden, about 1 minute. Drain.
5 Pour hot chicken stock into each bowl of noodles. Top noodles with some of the pickled radish, scallions, and deep-fried shallots. Serve accompanied by deep-fried dumplings and, if liked, chili sauce for dipping.

Singapore laksa with seafood and quail eggs

1 1/2 lb (750 g) fresh round rice-flour
(laksa) noodles
1 1/2 cups (150 g) bean sprouts
12 hard-boiled quail eggs, left whole,
or 4 hard-boiled hen eggs, quartered
12 fresh scallops, blanched until cooked
12 cooked medium shrimps, peeled
and deveined
4 pieces deep-fried dried tofu (*taufu
pok*), blanched in boiling water
30 seconds, sliced and drained of
excess oil

Gravy
2 tablespoons vegetable oil
8 large red chilies, processed to a paste
1 portion laksa paste (see below)
4 cups (1 liter) water
1 teaspoon salt
1 teaspoon sugar
2 cups (500 ml) coconut milk

Laksa paste
3 large onions (300 g), chopped
2 oz (60 g) galangal, chopped
6 cloves garlic, chopped
3 oz (90 g) fresh ginger, chopped
3 stems lemongrass, sliced
4–5 large red chilies, chopped
1/4 cup (60 ml) vegetable oil
2–3 teaspoons chili powder
2 teaspoons turmeric powder
3 teaspoons coriander powder
3/4 cup (40 g) firmly packed long-
stemmed Vietnamese mint (laksa
leaf or polygonum)
2 teaspoons dried shrimp paste, toasted
3/4 cup (75 g) dried shrimps, soaked in
water to soften, ground to a fine powder

This sophisticated Singapore laksa contains scallops, shrimps, and quail eggs, as well as the usual bean sprouts, deep-fried dried bean curd, and a spicy hot coconut-milk gravy bathing fresh rice-flour noodles. Although often eaten as a hearty breakfast in Asia, this laksa is just as good for lunch.

1 First of all, make the laksa paste, which will be used in the gravy. Process the onion, galangal, garlic, ginger, lemongrass, and chilies to a smooth paste. Heat the oil, add the spice paste, and stir-fry over low-moderate heat until the moisture has dried up and the oil starts to separate, about 10 minutes. Add chili, turmeric, and coriander powders, and the laksa leaves and stir-fry 1 minute. Add the dried shrimp paste and stir-fry for a further 1 minute, then add the dried shrimp powder and stir-fry for a final 1 minute. Transfer laksa paste to a bowl and leave to cool.
2 To make the gravy, heat oil in a saucepan and add oil. Stir-fry the chili paste for 1 minute, then add the laksa paste and stir to mix well. Stir in the water, salt, and sugar. Bring to a boil, lower heat and simmer uncovered for 10 minutes. Add the coconut milk and bring almost to a boil, then remove from heat.
3 To serve, blanch the noodles 30 seconds, then drain and divide between 4 large bowls. Fill each with some of the hot gravy, then add bean sprouts, eggs, scallops, shrimps, and bean curd slices to each serving. Serve with a chili *sambal* and lime (see Note).

Note: If you cannot obtain fresh laksa noodles, use 10 oz (300 g) dried flat rice-flour noodles cooked according to the instructions on the packet. To make a quick chili *sambal* to accompany this dish, pound or process 6 seeded and chopped large red chilies together with 1 teaspoon toasted dried shrimp paste to form a smooth paste. Divide between 4 small bowls and add a small green lime to each for squeezing into the *sambal* to taste.

Antique *Fu* dog—Four Seasons Hotel Singapore

Vegetables in spicy coconut broth

4 tablespoons curry powder
2 teaspoons turmeric powder
1/4 cup (60 ml) water
1/4 cup (60 ml) vegetable oil
2–3 shallots, very finely chopped
4 cloves garlic, very finely chopped
1 tablespoon very finely chopped ginger
1 stem lemongrass, very finely chopped
6 cups (1 1/2 liters) coconut milk
1 teaspoon salt, or more to taste
2 medium red onions, quartered
4 medium potatoes, cubed
4 baby carrots, left whole
3 long beans or 8 green beans, cut in
　1 1/2-in (4-cm) lengths
1 small slender Asian eggplant
　(aubergine), quartered lengthways
4 large red chilies, left whole
4 small broccoli florets
4 small cauliflower florets
4 small okra (ladies' fingers), stem ends
　trimmed, left whole
4 very small tomatoes, left whole

A favorite way of cooking vegetables in many tropical countries is to simmer them in coconut milk. Vegetables are normally cut into bite-sized pieces, but in this recipe from Singapore, very small vegetables are left whole where possible. This is a simple recipe to prepare, using curry powder with garlic, shallots, ginger, and lemongrass as the seasoning. This makes a generous curry to serve with rice for a vegetarian meal.

1 Mix the curry and turmeric powders and water in a small bowl to make a paste. Set aside.
2 Heat oil in a large saucepan and add the shallots, garlic, ginger, and lemongrass. Stir-fry over low-moderate heat until fragant and softened, 3–4 minutes. Add prepared spice paste and stir-fry for 2 minutes.
3 Add coconut milk and salt. Bring to a boil, stirring frequently, then simmer uncovered for 2 minutes. Add the onions, potatoes, and carrot and simmer uncovered for 10 minutes. Add all remaining vegetables except the tomatoes and simmer for a further 10 minutes. Add the tomatoes and cook another 5 minutes, or longer if needed until all the vegetables are tender. Serve with steamed white rice.

Shrimp and calamari in a turmeric coconut sauce

6 1/2 oz (200 g) calamari or small squid, cut in a crosshatch pattern (see Note)

10 oz (300 g) medium raw shrimps, peeled and deveined, tail section left intact

1 small chayote (christophene or choko), about 5 oz (150 g), peeled and cut in 1/4-in (1/2-cm) strips, blanched 2 minutes, or 1 very small zucchini (courgette), skin left on, cut in 1/4-in (1/2-cm) strips, blanched 1 minute

5 oz (150 g) green beans, cut in 1 3/4-in (4-cm) lengths, blanched 1 minute

1 large red chili, seeded and julienned

1 large green chili, seeded and julienned

3/4 cup (185 ml) thick coconut milk

Salt to taste

Liberal grinding of black pepper

Sauce

7–10 large red chilies, seeds discarded, chopped

5–6 shallots, chopped

1 1/2 tablespoons finely chopped turmeric

2 teaspoons finely chopped galangal

1 1/2 teaspoons finely chopped fresh ginger

2 tablespoons vegetable oil

1 tablespoon tamarind pulp, soaked in 1/4 cup (60 ml) warm water, squeezed and strained to obtain juice

1 cup (250 ml) fish stock or light chicken stock

Seafood seems to have a special affinity for coconut milk sauces, but the spicy gravy bathing this dish of shrimp and calamari is not overwhelmingly rich, thanks to the addition of fish or chicken stock. Plenty of chilies, turmeric, galangal, and ginger are added to the sauce, but as the chili seeds are discarded, you get all the flavor with minimal heat. Serve this with steamed white rice and a tangy side salad and you have a delicious and satisfying meal.

1 Prepare the turmeric coconut sauce. Process the chilies, shallots, turmeric, galangal, and ginger in a spice grinder or blender until smooth. Heat the oil in a saucepan and add processed mixture. Stir-fry the sauce over low-moderate heat until fragrant, 4–5 minutes. Add the tamarind juice and fish stock, bring to a boil, then simmer until slightly thickened, about 10 minutes.

2 Reheat the sauce, then add the calamari, shrimps, vegetables, and chilies. Bring to a boil, then simmer uncovered for 2 minutes. Add the coconut milk and cook, stirring several times, for another 3 minutes. Taste and add salt and pepper if desired. Serve hot with steamed rice.

Note: To match a crosshatch pattern on the squid, cut bodies in half lengthways. Score the soft inside of the squid pieces with diagonal lines using a very sharp knife, taking care not to cut right through the flesh. Turn the piece of squid and score diagonally across the lines already made, resulting in a crisscross pattern. Cut each squid half into bite-sized pieces.

Executive Chef Marc Miron—Four Seasons Resort Bali

Steamed fish in lemongrass and cilantro broth

4 baby whole red garoupa, about 10 oz (300 g) each, or 1 whole 1 1/2–lb (750-g) red garoupa cleaned and scaled, or 4 8-oz (250-g) fillets

20 tiger lily buds (golden needles), about 2/3 oz (20 g), soaked for 5 minutes, ends discarded

1 scallion (spring onion), cut in 1 3/4-in (4-cm) lengths

4 dried *asam gelugor* slices, or 4 slices lime or lemon

2 2/3 oz (80 g) pickled Sichuan vegetable, thinly sliced

2 small green limes (kalamansi or *limau kesturi*), halved

4 red or green chilies, split lengthways, to garnish

Lemongrass and cilantro broth

6 lb (3 kg) flower crabs
3–5 red bird's-eye chilies
6 cloves garlic, peeled and left whole
4 shallots, peeled and left whole
5 stems lemongrass, bruised
1/2 cup (20 g) chopped fresh cilantro (coriander) leaves and stems
2 quarts (2 liters) water
Salt and white pepper to taste

Steamed fish is one of the highlights of Chinese cuisine, and for the best results, the fish must be absolutely fresh. In this recipe—which combines sour, fragrant tropical Asian seasonings with spicy Sichuan vegetable—fish for individual-sized portions are steamed in a delicate crab stock perfumed with lemongrass (see Note).

1 Prepare the lemongrass and cilantro broth first. Cut the crabs in half lengthways with a cleaver and remove the backs and spongy crab matter. Remove claws from the body and crack with a cleaver in several places. Cut each body half into 2–3 pieces, leaving the legs attached. Wash, drain thoroughly and pat completely dry. Put the crab pieces, chilies, garlic, shallots, and lemongrass on an oven tray and cook at 425°F (220°C, gas 7) for 3 minutes. Transfer to a large saucepan, add fresh cilantro leaves and water, and bring to a boil. Boil uncovered, pressing on the crab pieces from time to time, for 30 minutes, or until the liquid is reduced by half. Strain, pressing down firmly on the crab to obtain as much juice as possible. Add salt and pepper to taste.

2 If using four fish or fish fillets, divide the tiger lily buds, scallion, sliced *asam gelugor*, and Sichuan vegetable, under each fish in a wide, shallow bowl. If using one large fish, add all ingredients to the bowl and place the fish on top.

3 Pour in enough stock to cover the fish and place the bowl on top of a rack set in a wok, above the level of the boiling water. Cover the wok and steam over rapidly boiling water until the fish is cooked (the flesh should be white when tested with the point of a knife), 10–15 minutes (about 20 minutes for one large fish). Transfer to 4 plates, garnish with half a lime and a red or green chili, and serve immediately with steamed white rice.

Note: The crab-infused lemongrass and cilantro broth is truly delicious and well worth the time and effort required to prepare it but for a quick and easy alternative, replace the crabs and water with 2 cups (500 ml) light chicken or fish stock and 2 cups (500 ml) water.

Antique Chinese porcelain—Four Seasons Hotel Singapore

Pan-fried fish fillet with mango, noodle salad, and spicy dressing

1 large ripe firm mango
4 skinned boneless white fish fillets,
  such as black cod, garoupa or sea
  bass, about 5 oz (150 g) each
1 teaspoon salt
Liberal sprinkling white pepper
2 tablespoons cornstarch
3 tablespoons vegetable oil
Fresh sprigs Chinese parsley and dill,
  to garnish

Salad
8 oz (250 g) dried rice vermicelli,
  soaked about 30 minutes in warm
  water until soft, drained, and separated
1 small onion, halved lengthways, very
  finely sliced across
2 shallots, thinly sliced
1 1/2 tablespoons very finely shredded
  fresh young ginger
2–4 bird's-eye chilies, sliced
3 tablespoons finely chopped scallion
  (spring onion)
3 tablespoons finely chopped fresh
  cilantro (coriander) stems and leaves
  or mint leaves
1/3 cup (85 ml) fish sauce
2 1/2 tablespoons lime juice
4 teaspoons superfine (caster) sugar
1/4 teaspoon sesame oil

The sweetness, smooth texture, and fragrance of fresh mango is perhaps the most striking feature of this easily prepared recipe. Pan-fried fish is served on a bed of vermicelli, herb, and mango salad, which has a Thai accent in the dressing of fish sauce, chili, and lime. The refreshing flavors of this recipe make it ideal for a warm tropical evening.

1 To prepare the salad, bring a saucepan of water to a boil, add the drained vermicelli and cook just 1 minute. Drain and cool, then transfer to a bowl and add onion, shallots, ginger, chilies, scallion, and cilantro (or mint). Toss gently to mix.
2 Cut mango in half lengthways (cut around the stone), then use a spoon to scoop out the flesh from each half. Cut half the flesh into fine strips, and the remainder into 1/2-in (1-cm) dice.
3 Put fish sauce, lime juice, sugar, and sesame oil in a small bowl and stir until the sugar dissolves. Pour over the salad, add the mango strips, and toss gently to mix. Divide between 4 serving plates and set aside while preparing the fish.
4 Put the fish on a plate and sprinkle both sides with salt, pepper, and cornstarch, shaking fish to remove excess cornstarch. Heat oil in a skillet and cook the fish over high heat, turning, until golden brown on both sides and cooked through, about 6 minutes. Drain fish on paper towel, then place on top of each portion of salad. Garnish with the diced mango and dressing, and serve.

Maldivian fish and pineapple curry

4 tablespoons very finely chopped fresh
  ginger
2 tablespoons very finely chopped garlic
1 teaspoon salt
2 teaspoons turmeric powder
2 teaspoons lime juice
1 lb (500 g) skinned boneless white fish,
  cut in 1 1/2-in (3-cm) cubes
3 tablespoons vegetable oil
10 cardamom pods, slit and bruised
1 teaspoon brown mustard seed
1 teaspoon cumin seed
1 large onion, thinly sliced
12 in (30 cm) pandan (screwpine) leaf,
  raked with a fork, tied in a knot
12 curry leaves
2–3 teaspoons chili powder
1 teaspoon coriander powder
1 1/2 tablespoons water
1 large ripe tomato, sliced
1 3/4 cups (435 ml) coconut milk
5 oz (150 g) fresh pineapple cubes
Salt to taste
1 medium green chili, sliced, to garnish

This curry has a lovely combination of flavors, with cubes of fish simmered in a richly spiced curry gravy softened with coconut milk, and fresh pineapple adding fragrance and a sweet-sour tang. Any fish with firm-textured white flesh would be suitable for this curry.

1 Pound or process ginger, garlic, and salt together to make a paste. Mix half this paste with the turmeric powder and lime juice, then transfer to a bowl and add fish, tossing gently to coat all over. Set aside. Retain the remaining paste.
2 Heat oil in a saucepan and add cardamom, mustard, and cumin seeds and stir-fry over high heat until they pop. (Known as *baghaar*, this method of dropping whole spices into hot oil until they pop gives the spices a more concentrated flavor.) Remove some of the spices and oil and set aside to garnish the cooked dish. Add onion, pandan, and curry leaves to the saucepan and stir-fry until the onion is light brown, 3–4 minutes. Add remaining ginger-garlic paste and stir-fry for 2 minutes.
3 Combine the chili and coriander powders, and the water in a small bowl, mixing to make a paste. Add to the pan and stir-fry until fragrant for 2 minutes.
4 Add the tomato and cook uncovered, stirring several times, until very soft, about 5 minutes. Add coconut milk gradually, scraping the bottom of the pan to dislodge any spices. Bring to a boil, stirring, then add the marinated fish and pineapple and simmer until fish is cooked, 6–7 minutes. Taste and add salt if desired. Discard pandan leaf, garnish with chili and reserved fried spices, and serve hot with steamed white rice.

Spices are dropped into hot oil to release their flavors

Wok-fried clams with chili, Chinese sausage, and daikon sprouts

1/4 cup (60 ml) vegetable oil
6–8 cloves garlic, very finely chopped
4 shallots, very finely chopped
1–2 large red chilies, very finely chopped
4 lb (2 kg) fresh clams, washed and drained
2 Chinese dried sausages (*lap cheong*)
1 can (13 oz or 400 g) tomatoes, blended to a purée
1 teaspoon coarsely ground black pepper
2 tablespoons chopped fresh cilantro (coriander) leaves
1/4 cup *daikon* or other radish sprouts
2 limes, halved

This quickly made dish has an unusual fragrance and touch of sweetness, thanks to the rose wine used to make Chinese dried sausages. A mixture of garlic, shallots, and chilies is briefly stir-fried, then the clams, sausages, tomato purée, black pepper, and cilantro are added. Just stir until all the clams are opened, garnish with radish sprouts and serve with crusty bread for mopping up the excellent sauce.

1 Heat oil in a wok, then add garlic, shallots, and chili. Stir-fry over moderate heat until softened, 2–3 minutes. Add the clams and sausages, increase heat, and stir-fry 1 minute.
2 Add the tomato purée, pepper, and cilantro leaf and cook, stirring frequently, until the clams have all opened, removing each clam to a serving dish as it opens to prevent them from over-cooking. Discard any clams which have not opened, add the sauce to the serving dish, and garnish with the *daikon* sprouts and a lime half.

Executive Chef Martin Awyong—Four Seasons Hotel Singapore

Ginger-poached chicken breast on mushroom medley

4 skinless chicken breasts, each about
  5 oz (150 g)
2–3 cups (500–750 ml) chicken stock,
  preferably homemade
4 in (10 cm) fresh ginger, peeled and
  bruised
4 cilantro (coriander) roots
Salt and white pepper to taste
6 1/2 oz (100 g) watercress sprigs
1 medium tomato, peeled and finely
  diced
2 tablespoons finely chopped chives

Mushroom medley
2 tablespoons olive oil
1 tablespoon vegetable oil
2 cloves garlic, smashed and chopped
1 2/3 oz (50 g) *shiitake* mushrooms,
  sliced
3 1/2 oz (100 g) *shimeji* mushrooms
1 2/3 oz (50 g) *nameko* mushrooms
1 2/3 oz (50 g) long golden *enoki*
  mushrooms
1/4 teaspoon salt
Freshly ground black pepper to taste
2 tablespoons mushroom oyster sauce,
  or regular oyster sauce

This recipe features a mixture of meaty fresh *shiitake* (more familiar in their dried version as dried black mushrooms), delicate little *nameko* and *shimeji* mushrooms and long slender golden *enoki*. These are stir-fried and served together with chicken breasts poached in ginger-flavored stock for a light, low-fat gourmet meal. Although Asian mushrooms are becoming increasingly available around the world, other types of mushrooms may be substituted if necessary.

1 Put the chicken breasts, stock, ginger, and cilantro roots in a saucepan and bring almost to a boil. Taste and add salt and pepper if desired. Cover the pan and poach over minimum heat, with the water just below simmering stage, until the chicken is cooked, about 20 minutes. Remove the pan from the heat but leave the chicken in the stock.
2 Prepare the mushroom medly. Heat both lots of oil in a wok and add the garlic. Stir-fry over high heat 10 seconds, then add the *shiitake* mushrooms and stir-fry 1 minute. Add the remaining mushrooms and stir-fry until cooked, about 2 minutes. Season with salt, pepper, and oyster sauce, stir well, then divide between 4 plates.
3 Add a warm chicken breast to each plate, spoon over some of the sauce, and garnish with watercress and tomatoes. Sprinkle over the chives and serve immediately.

Note: If not all these Asian mushrooms are available, choose a mixture of other fresh mushrooms such as straw mushrooms, oyster mushrooms, Swiss brown mushrooms, or portobello mushrooms; the use of canned mushrooms is not recommended. If liked, the remaining ginger-flavored chicken stock could be used as a soup to accompany the chicken; add some sliced scallion (spring onion) or cubes of silken tofu.

Hainanese chicken rice with pandan rice balls

4 pieces pandan (screwpine) leaf, each about 12 in (30 cm) long, raked with a fork and tied in a knot
2 in (5 cm) fresh ginger, peeled and bruised
6 cloves garlic, skins left on, bruised
3 quarts (3 liters) water
1 teaspoon salt
1 teaspoon black peppercorns
1 small chicken (2 lb or 1 kg), fat from inside of chest cavity reserved for rice
1/2 carrot, very finely julienned
1 medium red chili, sliced
1/2 small cucumber, cut in 1-in (2 1/2-cm) julienne
4 limes
2 scallions (spring onions), cut in 1-in (2 1/2-cm) lengths
1/4 cup (60 ml) dark soy sauce

Pandan rice balls
8 pieces pandan (screwpine) leaves, each about 12 in (30 cm) long, chopped
1/4 cup (60 ml) water
2 teaspoons reserved chicken fat
1/3 cup (85 ml) vegetable oil
2 1/4 in (6 cm) fresh ginger, peeled and bruised
5 cloves garlic, skin left on, bruised
5 shallots, peeled and bruised
2 cups (400 g) rice, washed and well drained
4 cups (1 liter) water
Pinch of salt

Chili sauce
1/2 teaspoon salt
6 large red chilies, chopped
5–6 cloves garlic, chopped

Ginger sauce
2 tablespoons finely chopped fresh ginger
1/4 teaspoon rice vinegar
1 tablespoon water

Stir-fried *choy sum*
1 tablespoon vegetable oil
2 teaspoons very finely chopped garlic
2 tablespoons oyster sauce
1/4 cup (60 ml) water
13 oz (400 g) Chinese flowering cabbage (*choy sum*), cut in 3-in (8-cm) lengths

A Hainanese classic that is one of Singapore's most popular dishes, chicken rice has several components: poached chicken; rice cooked with a touch of chicken fat; and hot chili and ginger sauces with dark soy sauce and ginger purée for adding to taste. In this recipe, the chicken and rice are both flavored with fragrant pandan leaf—a distinctly Singaporean touch—and served with stir-fried *choy sum*.

1 Prepare the chicken first. Put pandan leaf, ginger, garlic, water, salt, and pepper into a saucepan and bring to a boil. Add chicken, reduce heat until water is barely simmering, and cook until done, 50–60 minutes. Remove chicken and plunge into a bowl of iced water. Leave for 1 minute, then drain chicken and pat dry. Remove the flesh and discard the skin and bones. Cut chicken into bite-sized pieces.

2 To prepare the rice, process pandan leaves and water until the leaves are very finely ground and the liquid has turned green. Pour the mixture into a sieve set over a bowl and press with the back of a spoon to obtain the pandan juice. Set aside.

3 Put the chicken fat and oil in a saucepan and heat. Add the ginger, garlic, and shallots and stir-fry over low-moderate heat until fragrant, about 3 minutes. Add the drained rice and stir until it is well coated with the mixture, about 2 minutes. Add the water and salt, then bring to a boil and cook, uncovered, over high heat until the rice is almost dry and "craters" have formed in the surface, about 5 minutes. Pour over the pandan juice, then transfer to an oven-proof bowl with a lid and cook in the oven at 325°F (160°C, gas 3) for 30 minutes. Discard the pandan, ginger, garlic, and shallots. Using two large spoons or your hands (protected by rubber gloves), mold the rice into large balls.

4 While rice is cooking, make the chili and ginger sauces by processing or blending all the ingredients for each recipe. Transfer to 8 individual sauce bowls and set aside.

5 If you wish to serve stir-fried *choy sum*, heat 1 teaspoon of the oil in a small saucepan and add the garlic. Stir-fry until fragrant, about 10 seconds, then add the oyster sauce and water. Stir and set aside. Heat remaining oil in a wok and add the vegetable. Stir-fry over high heat until just cooked, about 2 minutes, sprinkling with a little water if it starts to stick and burn. Pour over the reserved oyster sauce and garlic, mix and immediately transfer to a serving plate.

6 To serve, place some carrot, red chili, cucumber, lime, and scallion on 4 plates and divide the chicken between the plates. Serve the rice balls and *choy sum* on separate plates. Transfer the dark soy sauce to sauce bowls and serve, allowing each person to add soy sauce to taste to their chili and ginger sauces.

Note: If you prefer to serve a simpler, lower-fat version of this rice, reduce the oil to 1 tablespoon, and use only 3 cups (750 ml) water. Cook the rice until almost dry, add the pandan juice, then instead of transferring the rice to the oven, cover the saucepan with a lid and cook over very low heat, 10 minutes. Wipe the inside of the lid, fluff up the rice with a fork, replace lid and stand another 10–15 minutes. Discard seasonings and serve as for normal rice rather than shaping it into balls. The rice can be cooked without pandan leaves if they are not available.

Coconut, palm honey, and pandan ice cream

1 3/4 cup (435 ml) milk
3/4 cup (185 ml) cream
12 in (30 cm) pandan (screwpine) leaf,
  raked with a fork, tied in a knot, or a
  few drops of pandan essence
4 egg yolks
3/4 cup (70 g) coconut milk powder
3 oz (90 g) palm honey or 1/3 cup
  (70 g) finely chopped palm sugar or
  soft brown sugar
4 slices finely shaved fresh coconut
1 tablespoon toasted shredded
  (desiccated) coconut

This sinfully delicious ice cream is so satisfying that just a couple of scoops will be enough to make the perfect conclusion to any meal. Milk, cream, and eggs are enriched with coconut milk powder and flavored with fragrant pandan and either palm honey or palm sugar.

1 Put milk, cream, and pandan leaf into a saucepan and bring slowly almost to boiling point, stirring constantly. Remove from the heat and stand 15 minutes. Discard pandan leaf.
2 Beat egg yolks and coconut milk powder together in a bowl until mixed, then slowly pour in a little of the hot milk mixture, stirring all the time. Return this to the milk mixture in the pan; add palm sugar at this stage if using this as a substitute for palm honey. Cook over low heat, stirring constantly, until the mixture thickens slightly, about 3 minutes. Pour through a sieve into a bowl, cool, then refrigerate 30 minutes. Stir in the palm honey, if using, then freeze in an ice cream maker. Transfer to a covered container and keep in the freezer until required.
3 Alternatively, transfer the mixture to a metal cake tin, cover with aluminum foil and freeze until icy around the edges, about 1 1/2 hours. Transfer to a food processor and blend to break up. Return the mixture to the tin, cover and freeze until firm, about 2 hours.
4 Transfer from the freezer to the refrigerator about 30 minutes before serving to soften slightly. Garnish with the shaved and toasted coconut.

Traveling by local ferry—Four Seasons Resort Maldives

Passionfruit cheese cake

2 1/2 teaspoons powdered gelatine
3 tablespoons hot water
8 oz (250 g) cream cheese
1/2 cup (125 g) superfine (caster) sugar
2 egg yolks
1/4 cup (60 ml) milk
1 1/4 cups (300 ml) whipping cream,
  whipped

Base
1 cup (200 g) butter, diced
1/2 cup (100 g) confectioners' (icing)
  sugar
1 egg white
1/2 teaspoon vanilla essence
2 cups (250 g) all-purpose (plain) flour
1/2 cup (50 g) rolled oats

Passionfruit topping
1/2 cup (125 ml) water
1/2 cup (125 ml) bottled passionfruit
  sauce or fresh passionfruit pulp
1 teaspoon powdered agar agar
Sugar to taste

Several varieties of passionfruit (a South American native) grow in the tropics, adding their wonderful perfume to a variety of dishes. This cheese cake, with a base containing rolled oats for a pleasantly firm texture, is covered by sweetened cream cheese enriched with egg yolk and combined with whipped cream and gelatine. When the cream cheese layer has chilled and set, it is topped with a glaze of passionfruit. This self-indulgent dessert provides plenty for second helpings.

1 To prepare the base, beat butter and sugar together until the sugar has dissolved. Stir in the egg white and vanilla, then fold in flour and oats. Mix well, then press into a rectangular cake tin about 5 x 10 1/2 in (12 x 26 cm). Refrigerate 30 minutes and, towards the end of the 30 minutes, preheat oven to 340°F (170°C, gas 3 1/2). Bake in preheated oven for 20 minutes, until set and cooked then remove and leave to cool.
2 Sprinkle the gelatine over the water and leave to soften and swell. Stir to mix well and set aside. Process the cream cheese and sugar to mix, then add the egg yolks, milk, and gelatine mixture. Process until smooth. Transfer to a bowl and use a spatula to fold in the whipped cream. Spread evenly over the cooled base. Refrigerate until set, 2–3 hours.
3 When cake is set, make the passionfruit topping. Combine all ingredients in a small saucepan and bring to a boil, stirring. Simmer 1 minute, then transfer to a bowl to cool for 10 minutes; do not leave for any longer as it will start to set. Spoon the topping evenly over the cheese cake and return to the refrigerator for 10–15 minutes to set firmly.

Passionfruit

Soy milk pannacotta with tropical fruit and pandan sauce

1 teaspoon powdered agar agar
1 1/3 cups (335 ml) soy milk
1 cup (250 ml) fresh milk
Superfine (caster) sugar to taste

Fruit garnish
4 oz (125 g) fresh papaya balls
4 oz (125 g) fresh mango balls
4 oz (125 g) fresh dragon fruit balls

Pandan sauce
1 1/2 cups (375) ml) fresh milk
3 pandan leaves, each about 12 in
(30 cm) long, raked with a fork, tied in
a knot, or pandan essence to taste
3 tablespoons superfine (caster) sugar
2 egg yolks

This lovely dessert uses milk made from soya beans, together with fresh milk and agar agar, to set it into milky jellies. The garnish of tropical fruit balls adds color and freshness, while the fragrant pandan-flavored custard brings the tropics to the table. Try to use unflavored soy milk if possible; look in your supermarket or health foodstore.

1 First prepare the pandan-flavored sauce. Put the milk and pandan leaves in a saucepan and bring slowly to a boil, stirring frequently. Simmer, uncovered, 1 minute, then remove from the heat, cover and leave to infuse 10 minutes. Pour through a sieve, squeezing pandan leaves to obtain maximum liquid and flavor. Discard the leaves.
2 Whisk the sugar and eggs yolks in a small bowl, then pour in one-third of the milk, stirring constantly. Put this and the remaining milk back in the pan and cook over low-moderate heat, stirring constantly, until the mixture thickens slightly and coats the back of a spoon. Cool, then transfer to a jug before using.
3 Sprinkle the powdered agar agar on 1/4 cup (60 ml) of the soy milk, and leave until it softens, about 5 minutes. Put the remaining soy milk and fresh milk in a saucepan and bring slowly to a boil, stirring. Add the agar agar mixture and sugar to taste (this will depend on whether the soy milk is sweetened). Return to a boil over low-moderate heat, stirring constantly.
4 Pour into 4 3-in (7-cm) hemispherical molds or glass bowls and leave to cool, then refrigerate for 1–2 hours to chill thoroughly. Unmold onto 4 serving plates. Arrange the fruit balls around each portion of pannacotta and serve with the jug of the pandan-flavored sauce for adding to taste.

Note: If you cannot obtain pandan leaves, prepare an equally delicious vanilla ginger sauce by substituting 1 2/3 oz (50 g) chopped fresh ginger and a 3-in (7-cm) length of split vanilla bean for the pandan leaves.

Dragon fruit

tropical night

After a brilliant sunset — when the sky is aflame with orange and red and gold, before slowly fading through deep purple to inky black — the full beauty of a tropical evening is upon you. A new chorus of insects takes over from those that have kept busy throughout the day, and the sun gives way to the moon, which drips silver from the coconut fronds.   The freshness that comes with the evening sharpens the appetite. There is plenty of time to spend on the preparation and leisurely enjoyment of food that celebrates the end of a wonderful day.   Salads, soups, and other starters include spicy beef broth with bean sprouts, white radish, and crispy shallots; tomato and lentil soup; and spinch *kofta* in eggplant purée.   Composite dishes may take longer to prepare, but the resulting range of flavors makes them well worth the effort. *Nasi campur*, literally "mixed rice," is the name given in Indonesia and Malaysia to a meal of rice with various side dishes of meat, chicken, vegetables, and spicy condiments. Our version has a wonderful herb and coconut-flavored rice as the centerpiece, with spicy *rendang* beef, stir-fried chicken, crunchy fermented soybean cake, and a wonderful mixed vegetable and fresh coconut salad.   Another composite dish is the Indian Muslim *biryani*. We offer this fragrant layered rice dish with a filling of spicy shrimps; saffron, cardamom, and other heady spices make this a memorable meal.   Our fish dishes run the gamut from spiced tuna steaks with an exciting citrus salsa to sharpen the palate, to a Spice Islands' favorite adapted for fish fillets in the baby snapper fillet with spicy chili, ginger, and tomato relish; and grilled whole snapper. But the ultimate in spicy seafood is surely Singapore's famous chili crab, with meaty crab pieces swimming in a rich, thick tomato-chili sauce. Serve with French bread to mop up every drop of delicious sauce.   Meat lovers will delight in the Vietnamese black pepper beef, *tandoori* lamb, pork back ribs, and a variation of a Dutch-Indonesian classic, *semur*, featuring grilled beef marinated with coriander.   To ensure sweet dreams, finish with a baked coconut cream custard, or retire with the taste of the tropics still lingering after a pineapple crumble.

Tomato and lentil soup

3/4 cup (125 g) yellow lentils, washed and drained
3/4 cup (125 g) red lentils, washed and drain
1 lb (500 g) ripe tomatoes, peeled and chopped
Salt and freshly ground black pepper to taste
Oil for deep-frying
1 1/4 oz (40 g) curd cheese (*paneer*) or baked ricotta, cut in 4 slices
Crisp-fried curry leaves, to garnish
Fresh cilantro (coriander) leaves, to garnish

Stock
1 small carrot, coarsely chopped
1/2 medium onion, chopped
1/2 white part of a leek, chopped
1/2 stalk celery, chopped
1 teaspoon black peppercorns
3 cloves
3/4 in (2 cm) cinnamon stick
1/3 cup (15 g) chopped fresh cilantro (coriander) leaves and stems
1/4 cup (10 g) chopped mint leaves and stems
4 cups (1 liter) water
1/2 teaspoon salt

This pleasant, mild soup has definite Indian overtones, although soup is rarely part of a meal in India. A mixture of yellow and red lentils and tomatoes are simmered in freshly made vegetable stock, lightly flavored with spices and herbs. This is an ideal starter to any meal, or is good as part of a light lunch if served with Indian or French bread, followed by a salad.

1 To prepare the stock, put all the ingredients in a large saucepan. Bring to a boil, cover, lower heat and simmer 45 minutes. Strain, pressing down with a wooden spoon to obtain the maximum liquid. Discard the solids.
2 Clean the saucepan and return the stock together with the lentils. Return to a boil, cover, lower heat, and simmer until the lentils are very soft, about 15 minutes.
3 Add the tomatoes and cook until very soft, 10–12 minutes. Push the soup through a fine strainer, then process in a blender until smooth. Check and add salt and pepper to taste.
4 Heat oil in a small pan and deep-fry the sliced *paneer* until golden brown. Drain on paper towel. Transfer soup to 4 bowls, and garnish each with a slice of the *paneer* and accompany, if liked, by deep-fried *pappadum*. Transfer soup to 4 bowls, add a slice of *paneer* to each bowl, and garnish with crisp-fried curry leaves, black pepper, and cilantro.

Note: A good alternative garnish to the deep-fried curd cheese would be 1 tablespoon thick plain yogurt with a sprinkle of cumin powder and a sprig of fresh cilantro (coriander) leaves on top of each serving.

Pappadum basket

Spicy beef broth with bean sprouts, radish, and crispy shallots

5 cups (1 1/4 liters) beef stock, preferably homemade
2 stems lemongrass, bruised and cut in 1 1/2-in (4-cm) lengths
2 *salam* leaves (if unavailable, omit)
2 teaspoons finely chopped palm sugar
1 tablespoon tamarind pulp
Salt and white pepper to taste

Spice paste
5 shallots, chopped
4–6 cloves garlic, chopped
2 tablespoons finely chopped galangal
1 teaspoon finely chopped turmeric
1/2 teaspoon dried shrimp paste
4 candlenuts, chopped
2 tablespoons vegetable oil

Garnishes
10 oz (300 g) seared tender beef (rump or fillet), thinly sliced
8–12 thin slices long white radish (*daikon*), blanched
1 small carrot, thinly sliced, blanced
1 medium red chili, finely chopped
4 kaffir lime leaves, very finely shredded
4 teaspoons crisp-fried shallots
1 cup (75 g) loosely packed bean sprouts, washed and drained, straggly tails discarded
1 scallion (spring onion), finely chopped, to garnish

This satisfying soup is inspired by the hot, fragrant *soto* Padang from the west coast of Sumatra, Indonesia. Beef stock is simmered with an aromatic paste, herbs, sour tamarind, and a touch of palm sugar, then strained and served with paper-thin slices of seared beef, crunchy bean sprouts, white radish, and crisp-fried shallots. Serve with steamed rice and a mixed vegetable dish for a complete and healthy meal.

1 Prepare the spice paste by processing all ingredients except oil in a spice grinder. Add a little of the oil if needed to keep the mixture turning. Heat the remaining oil in a large saucepan and add spice paste. Stir-fry over low heat until fragrant, 4–5 minutes. Add the beef stock, lemongrass, *salam* leaves (if using), palm sugar, and tamarind pulp. Bring to a boil, stirring several times. Cover, lower heat, and simmer 45 minutes. Strain through a sieve, pressing down with the back of a spoon to extract maximum liquid.
2 Reheat soup, taste and add salt and pepper if required. Divide between 4 soup bowls, add a little of each of the garnishes to each portion and serve hot.

Note: To slice kaffir lime leaves quickly and easily, roll up firmly, from stem to tip end rather than side to side. Place on a cutting board and slice very finely with a sharp knife, discarding the central rib.

Spinach kofta with eggplant purée

1 tablespoon vegetable oil
1 teaspoon cumin seeds
1/2 small onion, finely chopped
1 teaspoon very finely chopped garlic
1 teaspoon very finely chopped fresh
  ginger
13 oz (400 g) potato, boiled and
  mashed
1 1/4 oz (40 g) homemade curd cheese
  (*paneer*) or baked ricotta, grated
6 1/2 oz (200 g) spinach leaves,
  blanched 1 minute, drained, squeezed
  dry and finely chopped
1/2 teaspoon *garam masala*
1/2 teaspoon salt
3 tablespoons chickpea flour (*besan*)
Vegetable oil for deep-frying
1 tomato, cut in wedges
1 red onion, cut in wedges
4 whole green chilies
4 sprigs fresh cilantro (coriander), to
  garnish
4 deep-fried *pappadum* (optional)

Eggplant purée
1 small eggplant (aubergine), about 8 oz
  (250 g)
1/2 teaspoon very finely chopped garlic
2 teaspoons curry powder
1/4 cup (60 ml) plain yogurt
1/4 teaspoon salt
1 tablespoon chopped fresh cilantro
  (coriander) leaves
1/2 small tomato, finely diced

This dish consists of two tasty vegetable combinations: *kofta* (balls made from spinach, potato, and a little curd cheese or *paneer*) and an accompaniment of eggplant purée, with spicy crunchy *pappadum* for textural contrast. Served with *basmati* rice, a salad, and a tangy chutney, this makes a satisfying vegetarian meal, although you could always add grilled meat or poultry.

1 Prepare the eggplant purée. Cook the eggplant under a very hot grill or over charcoal, turning until the skin turns black and the inside is tender. Cut eggplant in half and scoop out the flesh. Chop the flesh finely and mix with all the other ingredients. Set aside.
2 To make the spinach balls, heat the oil in a pan and cook the cumin seeds until they begin to crackle. Add onion, garlic, and ginger and stir-fry over low-moderate heat until softened, about 3 minutes. Add the potato, cheese, spinach, *garam masala* and salt. Stir-fry for 2 minutes, mixing thoroughly. Transfer to a bowl and stir in the chickpea flour. Cool, then shape into balls about 1 1/4 in (3 cm) in diameter.
3 Heat oil in a wok and when very hot, cook the *kofta*, turning until golden brown all over, about 2 minutes. Drain on paper towel and serve accompanied by the eggplant purée. Garnish with tomato, red onion, chili, cilantro, and, if desired, some *pappadum*.

Spinach balls

Deep-fried tofu with vegetables and peanut sauce

Vegetable oil for deep-frying
13 oz (400 g) firm tofu, dried with
  paper towel
2 cups (150 g) bean sprouts, washed
  and drained
1/2 cup (50 g) finely julienned cucumber
1/2 cup (50 g) finely julienned carrot
1 medium red chili, finely julienned
1/2 cup (40 g) green pea shoots (*dau
  miao*)
1/2 cup (10 g) torn yellow frisée lettuce,
  or 4 small leaves cos lettuce
1 scallion (spring onion), cut in 1 1/4-in
  (3-cm) lengths
2 tablespoons coarsely ground
  dry-roasted peanuts

Peanut sauce
1 large red chili, thinly sliced
4 cloves garlic, finely chopped
2 tablespoons finely chopped palm
  sugar
4 teaspoons white vinegar
3 tablespoons dark soy sauce
1/2 cup (125 ml) water
2/3 cup (100 g) peanuts, dry-roasted,
  skinned, and finely ground

This is a Singaporean and Malaysian hawker favorite, eaten at food stalls as a snack or appetizer. Firm cakes of tofu are deep-fried then tossed with a mixture of refreshing bean sprouts, cucumber, carrot, pea shoots, lettuce, and with a thick sauce made of crushed peanuts, dark soy sauce, palm sugar, chili, garlic, and a touch of vinegar.

1 Prepare the peanut sauce. Process all ingredients together to make a thick sauce, then transfer to a large bowl. Set aside.
2 Heat the oil and deep-fry the tofu over high heat until crisp and golden on all sides, 3–4 minutes. Drain on paper towel, then cut tofu into 1 1/4-in (3-cm) chunks.
3 Transfer the tofu, bean sprouts, cucumber, carrot, chili, pea shoots, and lettuce to the bowl of peanut sauce and toss gently to mix thoroughly. Transfer to 4 serving dishes and top each portion with a little scallion and ground peanuts.

Note: Firm tofu may also be pan-fried in a little oil but the result will not be so crispy.

Sunday brunch—Four Seasons Hotel Singapore

Sautéed mushrooms with dried chilies and cashew nuts

16 dried monkey head mushrooms
(3 1/2 oz or 100 g dried monkey
heads to yield 11 1/2 oz or 350 g
softened monkey heads) (see Note)
1/4 cup finely chopped fresh young
ginger
1/4–1/3 cup (60–85 ml) water
2 tablespoons vegetable oil
4 cloves garlic, thinly sliced
3/4 in (2 cm) fresh ginger, thinly sliced
2 dried red chilies, cut in 3/4-cm (2-cm)
lengths
1 scallion (spring onion), cut in 3-cm
(1 1/4-in) lengths
2 teaspoons potato starch or cornstarch
2 tablespoons lightly fried cashew nuts
1 teaspooon white sesame seeds
Shredded lemon zest to garnish

Sauce
1/2 cup (125 ml) chicken stock
2 tablespoons chili sauce
2 tablespoons Maggi seasoning
1 tablespoon Chinese black vinegar
1 tablespoon dark soy sauce
2 teaspoons oyster sauce
1 teaspoon sugar
1 teaspoon sesame oil
Pinch of Chinese five-spice powder

This dish was inspired by a special type of Chinese mushroom known as *hou tou gu*—literally "monkey head mushroom"—due to its short spiky hair. If you are unable to locate these mushrooms in a Chinese grocery store then use regular dried black mushrooms instead.
A tangy sauce is added to the mushrooms after they have been blanched in ginger juice, and stir-fried with chili, with a scattering of crunchy cashew nuts adding the final touch.

1 Wash mushrooms and soak in warm water to soften slightly. Squeeze out some of the liquid. Trim off the hard stems and cut into bite-sized pieces.
2 Process the 1/4 cup chopped ginger and water until the ginger is very finely ground, adding a little more water if you are not able to obtain juicy young ginger. Pour mixture into a sieve and press firmly with the back of a spoon to extract the ginger water. Bring the ginger water to a boil and blanch the mushrooms for 1 minute. Remove and squeeze out some of the liquid, then briefly pan-fry in a little oil over high heat to seal the moisture. Remove and drain on paper towel. Set aside.
3 To prepare the sauce, combine all the ingredients in a small bowl, stirring to dissolve the sugar. Set aside.
4 Heat the oil in a wok and add garlic, sliced ginger, and dried chilies. Stir-fry over moderate heat until the garlic turns golden, then add the mushrooms and scallion and stir-fry 30 seconds. Add the prepared sauce and cook, stirring, for 1 minute. Add the cornstarch mixture and stir until the sauce thickens and clears, about 30 seconds.
5 Transfer to a serving dish, and scatter with the cashew nuts and white sesame seeds. Garnish with lemon zest and serve immediately.

Note: If monkey head mushrooms are not available, substitute with dried black mushrooms and soak for 1/2 hour to soften, then boil in ginger water for about 10 minutes until tender.

Monkey head mushrooms

Maldivian vegetable curry

2 cups (500 ml) water
1 teaspoon salt
2 teaspoons turmeric powder
1 small potato, diced
1 small carrot, diced
1 cup (100 g) diced green beans
1 very small zucchini (courgette), diced
1/2 cup (100 g) green peas

Spice paste
2 tablespoons finely chopped ginger
1 teaspoon finely chopped garlic
3 tablespoons vegetable oil
10 cardamom pods, slit and bruised
1 teaspoon brown mustard seeds
2 teaspoons cumin seeds
2 medium onions, thinly sliced
8 in (20 cm) pandan (screwpine) leaf,
  raked with a fork, tied in a knot
12 curry leaves
1–2 teaspoons chili powder
2 teaspoons coriander powder
2 tablespoons water
2 small tomatoes, chopped
1 3/4 cups (435 ml) coconut milk
Additional salt to taste

In this recipe, a combination of diced vegetables (potatoes, carrots, peas, beans, and zucchini) is blanched and then simmered in a delightfully spiced sauce of coconut milk and tomato. This vegetable dish would be ideal served with grilled fish or meat, although for a vegetarian meal, you could double the amounts and serve it simply with rice and a side-salad of cucumbers in yogurt.

1 Bring water, salt, and 1 teaspoon of the turmeric powder to a boil in a saucepan. Add the carrot and potato and blanch 2 minutes. Remove vegetables with a slotted spoon and set aside. Add the beans, zucchini, and peas to the same water, and blanch for 1 minute only. Drain and set aside.
2 Pound or process ginger and garlic together to make a paste, adding a little of the oil if necessary. Set aside. Heat oil in a saucepan until very hot, then drop in the cardamom, and mustard and cumin seeds. When the spices pop, add onion, pandan, and curry leaves, and stir-fry until the onion is light brown, 3–4 minutes. Add ginger-garlic paste and stir-fry for 2 minutes.
3 Combine remaining 1 teaspoon turmeric, chili, and coriander powders, and water in a small bowl, mixing to make a paste. Add to the pan and stir-fry until fragrant, 2 minutes.
4 Add the tomatoes and cook uncovered, stirring several times, until very soft, about 5 minutes. Add coconut milk gradually, scraping the bottom of the pan to dislodge any spices. Bring to a boil, stirring, then add blanched vegetables and simmer uncovered until the vegetables are tender, about 10 minutes. Serve hot with steamed white rice.

An array of Indian spices

Scallop and squid salad

8–12 fresh scallops
4 small squid, peeled, bodies halved
   lengthways, cut in crosshatch pattern
   (see Note)
1/2 teaspoon salt
Liberal sprinkling white pepper
1 tablespoon olive oil
8 arugula or rocket leaves, washed and
   dried
2 kaffir lime leaves, very finely shredded
2 small onions, thinly sliced
2 tablespoons very finely julienned
   carrot
1 large red chili, halved across, finely
   shredded
1 teaspoon sesame seeds, toasted until
   golden

Dressing
1/3 cup (85 ml) plus 1 tablespoon fish
   sauce
3 tablespoons lime juice
2 teaspoons very finely chopped fresh
   cilantro (coriander) leaves
1 teaspoon sesame oil
1 large red chili, finely chopped
1 clove garlic, very finely chopped
1 teaspoon sugar
3 1/2 tablespoons extra virgin olive oil,
   or a combination of garlic and
   orange/lemon oils (see Note)
1 kaffir lime leaf, very finely shredded

Garlic oil
Scant 1/2 cup (100 ml) vegetable oil
6 cloves garlic, smashed
Salt and pepper to taste

Orange or lemon oil
2/3 cup (150 ml) vegetable oil
Zest of 1 lemon, or 3 1/2 tablespoons
   orange juice
1 bay leaf
Salt and pepper to taste

This salad is perfect for lunch, or for a starter at dinner, and the dressing is excellent poured over grilled whole fish.

1 Prepare the dressing by combining all the ingredients except the olive oil (or flavored oil) and kaffir lime leaf in a small bowl, stirring to dissolve the sugar. Put the olive (or flavored) oil in a separate bowl and add the fish sauce mixture a few drops at a time, whisking constantly until the dressing starts to emulsify and thicken. Keep adding the oil gradually until it is all absorbed, then stir in the lime leaf and set the dressing aside.
2 Sprinkle the scallops and squid on both sides with salt and pepper. Heat half the oil in a wok and stir-fry the scallops over very high heat until they turn white, about 1 minute. Remove and drain on paper towel. Add remaining oil and, when very hot, stir-fry the squid halves until they turn white, about 1 1/2–2 minutes. Remove and drain on paper towel.
3 Arrange aragula leaves, kaffir lime leaf, shallots, carrot, and chili on a serving plate. Add the scallops and squid, drizzle over the dressing and sprinkle with sesame seeds.

Note: To match a crosshatch pattern on the squid, cut bodies in half lengthways. Score the soft inside of the squid pieces with diagonal lines using a very sharp knife, taking care not to cut right through the flesh. Turn the piece of squid and score diagonally across the lines already made, resulting in a crisscross pattern. To make your own flavored oils, simply cook the ingredients over very slow fire until the oil is flavorful and aromatic then cool and bottle.

Peanut-crusted shrimps on green mango salad

24 medium-sized raw shrimps (about
  1 1/2 lb or 750 g)
4 candlenuts or almonds, chopped
3 cloves garlic, chopped
2 teaspoons finely chopped turmeric
1 tablespoon finely chopped aromatic
  ginger (*kencur/cekur*) or fresh ginger
1 egg, lightly beaten
1/2–3/4 cup (125–185 ml) water
1 cup (120 g) rice flour
1/3 cup (40 g) cornstarch
1/4 teaspoon white pepper
1/4 teaspoon coriander powder
2 teaspoons salt
3–4 kaffir lime leaves, very finely shredded
3/4 cup (125 g) dry-roasted peanuts,
  skins discarded, coarsely chopped
Vegetable oil for deep-frying
1/3 oz (10 g) dried *kway teow* noodles,
  broken in 2-in (5-cm) lengths, deep-
  fried in very hot oil until crisp
4 sprigs fresh cilantro (coriander) leaves

Green mango salad
3 unripe green mangoes, julienned to
  yield about 8 oz (250 g) flesh
4 pieces ripe but firm jackfruit, julienned,
  or additional 4 oz (125 g) green mango
2 large red chilies, seeded and finely
  julienned
1 tablespoon finely chopped fresh
  cilantro (coriander) leaves
1 tablespoon finely chopped mint leaves
1 tablespoon lime juice
1 tablespoon brown sugar
1 1/2 teaspoons fish sauce
4–6 small dried shrimps, processed to a
  powder

Shrimps dipped in a flavorful crunchy batter containing chopped peanuts are deep-fried in this unusual recipe. The accompanying salad of green mango and jackfruit has a sweet-sour tang and contrasts beautifully with the shrimps and the crisp garnish of deep-fried noodles.

1 To prepare the mango salad, combine all ingredients. Refrigerate salad in a covered container while preparing the shrimps.
2 Peel the shrimps, leaving the final section and the tail intact. Discard the heads and shells, and cut down the back of each shrimp to remove the dark vein. Set shrimps aside.
3 Process candlenuts, garlic, turmeric, and aromatic ginger until finely ground, adding a little water if needed to keep the mixture turning. Put spice paste in a bowl and whisk in 1/2 cup (125 ml) water and the beaten egg. Set aside.
4 Combine rice flour, cornstarch, pepper, coriander powder, salt, and lime leaves in a separate bowl, stirring well to mix. Slowly stir in the water and spice paste mixture, adding a little more water if needed to make a thick batter. Stir in the chopped peanuts.
5 Heat oil for deep-frying in a wok. When very hot, hold a shrimp by the tail and dip it in the peanut batter to coat all over. Carefully slip it into the hot oil and fry the shrimps, a few at a time, until crisp and golden brown, about 3 minutes. Drain on paper towel and keep warm while cooking the remainder.
6 Arrange some of the green mango salad on each dish, and garnish with the fried noodles and cilantro sprigs. Add 6 shrimps to each plate and serve immediately.

Note: Cut the dried *kway teow* noodles with scissors or break by hand, and do not soak before frying.

Grilled tiger prawns with vindaloo dip and morukku

12 giant tiger prawns, peeled and
  deveined, final tail section left intact
2 cups mixed salad greens and herbs,
  such as frisée lettuce, rocket, torn
  Romaine or cos lettuce, scallions
  (spring onions), and sprigs of fresh
  mint and cilantro (coriander)
Morukku, to garnish

Marinade
4 cloves garlic, chopped
3/4 in (2 cm) fresh ginger, chopped
1 teaspoon salt
2 teaspoons chili powder
1 teaspoon turmeric powder
1 1/2 tablespoons lime juice

Vindaloo dip
12–15 dried chilies, cut in 3/4-in (2-cm)
  lengths, seeds discarded if desired
2 teaspoons chopped fresh ginger
4 cloves garlic, chopped
1 teaspoon brown mustard seeds
1 teaspoon turmeric powder
1 teaspoon coriander seeds
1 teaspoon black peppercorns
1 teaspoon cumin seeds
1 teaspoon *garam masala*
1/2 cup (125 ml) vinegar
1/2 cup (125 ml) boiling water
2 tablespoons vegetable oil
2 tablespoons tomato paste
1 teaspoon sugar
1/2 teaspoon salt

Vinadaloo, a famous dish from Goa, on the west coast of India, is characterized by plenty of garlic, chilies, vinegar, and spices. In this modern version, a vindaloo dip is prepared separately rather than being cooked together with pork or chicken, and is served with marinated, grilled tiger prawns, and *morukku*, or spiced breadsticks.

1 Prepare the *vindaloo* dip. Combine chilies, ginger, garlic, and all the spices including the *garam masala* in a bowl. Add vinegar and water and leave to soak for 6 hours. Put the solids and just 1–2 tablespoons of the liquid in a food processor or blender and process to a smooth paste. Add remaining liquid and mix to blend in. Heat the oil in a small pan, then add the spice mixture and tomato paste. Bring to a boil, stirring, then cook very gently, uncovered, for 15 minutes. Stir in salt, then press the sauce through a sieve. Set aside.

2 Prepare the marinade by pounding or processing garlic, ginger, and salt to a paste. Transfer to a bowl and stir in chili powder, turmeric, and lime juice. Add the prawns and toss to coat well. Marinate in the refrigerator for 30 minutes.

3 Heat a charcoal grill. Cook prawns over high heat, turning to cook both sides, about 4 minutes on each side, depending on the size of the prawns. Place salad greens on a serving plate and arrange prawns on top. Reheat *vindaloo* sauce and serve as a dipping sauce. Serve immediately, and garnish with *morukku* (see Note).

Note: *Morukku*—the corkscrew-shaped, spiced breadsticks—are available from Indian grocers. To make your own, combine 50 g (1/3 cup) chick pea flour (*besan*), 50 g (1/3 cup plus 2 tablespoons) rice flour, 1 teaspoon cumin powder, 1/2 teaspoon chili powder, 1/2 teaspoon turmeric powder, 3/4 teaspoon salt, and 1/4 teaspoon baking powder in a bowl, mixing well. Finely chop 1 clove garlic and 1 thin slice ginger and process them with 2 teaspoons lime juice to a paste. Add to the flour mixture, then stir in sufficient water (about 1/3–1/2 cup or 85–125 ml) to make a fairly soft dough that can easily be pushed through a pastry (forcing) bag. Leave to stand 15 minutes, then heat oil in a wok until moderately hot. Put the dough into a pastry (forcing) bag fitted with a very small nozzle and pipe some of the dough directly into the hot oil in a circular motion. Cook until crisp and golden brown, about 3 minutes, then remove with a slotted spoon, and drain on paper towel.

Executive Chef Frank Ruidavet—Maldives

Shrimp biryani

1 lb 3 oz (600 g) raw shrimps, peeled
  and deveined
2 tablespoons vegetable oil
6 whole cardamom pods, slit and bruised
3 cloves
1 teaspoon cumin
2 1/2 in (6 cm) cinnamon stick
2 dried cinnamon (*tej pati*) or bay leaves
10 black peppercorns
2 large onions, thinly sliced
2 cloves garlic, smashed and chopped
1 teaspoon very finely chopped ginger
2 teaspoons chili powder
2 teaspoons *garam masala*
1 teaspoon coriander powder
1 teaspoon cumin powder
3 medium tomatoes, sliced
1/3 cup (85 ml) plain yogurt
2 tablespoons water
1/2 teaspoon salt
1 tablespoon finely chopped mint
1 tablespoon finely chopped fresh
  cilantro (coriander) leaves

Marinade for shrimps
1 tablespoon finely chopped garlic
2 teaspoons finely chopped ginger
1 teaspoon salt
2 teaspoons lime juice
1 teaspoon turmeric powder

Biryani rice
Pinch saffron strands
1 tablespoon hot milk
1 tablespoon vegetable oil
4 whole cardamom pods, slit and
  bruised
2 cloves
1 teaspoon cumin
2 dried cinnamon (*tej pati*) or
  bay leaves
2 in (5 cm) cinnamon stick
2 3/4 cups (685 ml) water
1 teaspoon salt
2 cups (400 g) Basmati rice, washed,
  soaked 30 minutes, drained

Garnish
1 1/2 tablespoons fried onion or
  deep-fried shallots
1 1/2 tablespoons cashew nuts, split in
  half lengthways, fried in a little butter
  until golden
1 1/2 tablespoons raisins, fried in a little
  butter until soft and swollen
1 tablespoon finely chopped mint
Fresh cilantro (coriander) sprigs to
  garnish

Biryani is a festive dish which requires three separate stages of preparation: cooking a spicy shrimp curry, preparing a fragrant *pilau*-style rice, and assembling the rice and shrimps to finish the *biryani* in the oven. Serve with the *ketchumbar* salad (page 161).

1 Put the shrimps in a bowl. To make the marinade, pound or process the garlic, ginger, and salt to a paste, then stir in the lime juice and turmeric powder. Add to the shrimps and mix well. Set aside to marinate 30 minutes.
2 To cook the marinated shrimps, heat the oil in a wok and add cardamom, cloves, cumin, cinnamon stick and cinnamon leaves, and peppercorns. Stir-fry for 2–3 minutes, then add onions and stir-fry until the onions start to brown, about 8 minutes. Add the garlic and ginger, stir-fry for 30 seconds, then add the chili powder, *garam masala,* and coriander and cumin powders. Stir-fry for 1 minute, then add tomatoes and cook until softened, 4–5 minutes. Add the marinated shrimps, yogurt, water, and salt, stirring to mix well. Simmer uncovered until shrimps are cooked, 4–5 minutes. Scatter with mint and cilantro.
3 To prepare the *biryani* rice, sprinkle the saffron on the hot milk and leave to soak for 15 minutes. Press on the strands to obtain maximum color, then set milk and saffron aside. Heat the oil in a saucepan and add the cardamom, cloves, cumin, cinnamon leaves, and cinnamon stick. Stir-fry for 2–3 minutes, then add water and salt and bring to a boil. Add rice, stir, then boil uncovered until the water has dried up and holes appear in the surface of the rice, about 8 minutes. Sprinkle saffron milk and strands over rice, cover and reduce heat to minimum. Cook another 5 minutes. Fluff up rice with a fork; set aside.
4 To finalize the dish, preheat oven to 350°F (180°C, gas 4). Spread half the rice in the bottom of a heat-proof dish with a firmly fitting lid. Spread the cooked shrimps on top, then cover the shrimps evenly with the remaining rice. Cover the dish and cook in preheated oven for 12–15 minutes.
5 To garnish the *biryani*, sprinkle with the fried shallots or onion, cashews, raisins, and mint. Serve, if liked, with plain yogurt or a cucumber *raita (page 172)*, *naan* bread (page 172), and *ketchumbar* salad (page 161).

Serene dining—Four Seasons Resort Maldives

Spiced tuna steaks with citrus salsa

4 tuna steaks, each 6–6 1/2 oz
  (180–200 g), about 1-in (2 1/2-cm)
  thick
1 teaspoon salt
2 teaspoons lime juice
4 cloves garlic, chopped
1 1/2 tablespoons curry powder
1–2 tablespoons vegetable oil
Pomegranate seeds, to garnish
  (optional)
Fresh cilantro (coriander) sprigs, to
  garnish

Citrus salsa
1 small mandarin
1 lemon
1 orange
1/4 pineapple
1/4 pink graprfruit
1/4 coconut, sliced
Sugar to taste

This recipe is incredibly easy but so good nobody will believe that it takes less than 5 minutes to prepare the fish, plus 1 hour marinating. The sweet and sour tang of the citrus salsa adds a delightful piquancy and freshness that complements the rich spicy tuna perfectly.

1 Put the fish on a plate and sprinkle both sides with salt and lime juice. Scatter one side with some of the garlic, then with some of the curry powder, pressing to make it adhere to the fish. Turn and season the second side with garlic and curry powder. Cover and marinate 1 hour in the refrigerator.
2 While tuna is marinating, prepare the citrus salsa. Peel all the fruit, and remove the membranes covering each segment. Combine the segments in a bowl, stirring to mix well. Taste and add sugar if necessary. Cover and refrigerate until serving time.
3 Heat a charcoal grill. Brush both sides of the fish with oil and cook, about 4 minutes on each side. Serve with the prepared salsa. Garnish with pomengranate seeds (if using) and cilantro.

Note: You may use any combination of citrus fruits, depending on what is available.

Cocktail menu—Four Seasons Resort Maldives

Baby snapper fillets with ginger, chili, and tomato relish

4 baby snapper, grouper or bream fillets,
   each around 6–6 1/2 oz (180–200 g)
1 teaspoon salt
Dash of white pepper
1 tablespoon finely chopped fresh
   cilantro (coriander) leaves
1/4 cup (60 ml) vegetable oil
8 cherry tomatoes, or 1 large tomato
   cut in 8 wedges
4 red or green bird's-eye chilies, left
   whole
8 sprigs lemon basil

Sauce
2 tablespoons vegetable oil
12–15 large red chilies, some or all of
   the seeds discarded, sliced
4–5 red or green bird's-eye chilies,
   sliced
8 cloves garlic
1 1/4 in (3 cm) fresh ginger, thinly sliced
2 stems lemongrass, cut in 3 pieces
2 kaffir lime leaves, edges torn
1 1/2 cups (375 ml) water
1/2 teaspoon salt

Inspired by the Indonesian Spice Islands' favorite, *ikan dabu-dabu*, this recipe for fried fish in chili sauce is particularly fragrant, thanks to the use of ginger, garlic, lemongrass, lemon basil, and kaffir lime leaves. You can always discard the chili seeds to reduce the heat if you prefer a milder version.

1 To prepare the sauce, heat oil in a small saucepan and add both lots of chilies, garlic, and ginger. Stir-fry over low heat until fragrant, 3–4 minutes. Add the lemongrass, lime leaves, water, and salt, and simmer 10 minutes. Discard lemongrass and lime leaves and process to a smooth sauce. Set aside.
2 Season both sides of the snapper fillets with salt, pepper, and cilantro leaves. Heat oil in a skillet, then sear the fish for 2 minutes on each side. Add the tomatoes and cook for a few seconds, shaking the pan. Pour in the sauce and add the whole bird's-eye chilies. Simmer gently for 3 minutes, then add the lemon basil sprigs. Continue simmering until the fish is cooked through, another 2–3 minutes, depending on the thickness of the fish. Serve hot with steamed white rice.

Rooftop lotus pond—Four Seasons Resort Bali at Sayan

Grilled whole snapper Tabanan-style

1 whole fresh snapper, weighing about
  3 lb (1 1/2 kg), cleaned and scaled
1/2 teaspoon salt
Liberal sprinkling white pepper
1 quantity shallot and lemongrass
  sambal (see page 167)
2 limes, halved, to garnish

Marinade
1/4 cup (60 ml) vegetable oil
8–10 shallots, sliced
4–5 cloves garlic, sliced
8–12 large red chilies, sliced
2 red or green bird's-eye chilies, sliced
1 1/2 tablespoons finely chopped
  galangal
2 small ripe tomatoes, chopped
2 teaspoons dried shrimp paste, toasted
3 stems lemongrass, finely chopped
2 *salam* leaves (optional)
1 teaspoon salt
1/4 teaspoon freshly ground black
  pepper
2 teaspoons lime juice

This marinated barbecued fish is named after the Tabanan area in southwest Bali, Indonesia, once the seat of a great raja. The marinade—a superb blend of shallots, garlic, chilies, aromatics, and herbs—gives the fish a heady fragrance and flavor which is further enhanced by the accompanying shallot and lemongrass *sambal*.

1 To prepare the marinade, heat oil in a small pan and add shallots and garlic. Stir-fry over low heat, 3 minutes, then add chilies, galangal, tomatoes, shrimp paste, lemongrass and *salam* leaves (if using). Cook uncovered, stirring occasionally, 10 minutes. Remove from heat, cool, then process until smooth. Transfer to a bowl and stir in salt, pepper, and lime juice.
2 Make 3–4 deep diagonal slashes on both sides of the fish, then sprinkle both sides with salt and pepper. Spread a little of the marinade inside the fish, then cover both sides with the remaining marinade, pushing it well into the cuts. Set fish aside to marinate 20–30 minutes.
3 Enclose the fish in a fish grill and cook over hot charcoal 10 minutes. Turn and continue cooking until the fish is thoroughly cooked, another 10–20 minutes. Test with the point of a knife to ensure the fish is white in the center before serving.
4 Accompany the fish with shallot and lemongrass *sambal* (page 167) and garnish with lime halves.

Note: To reduce the heat of the marinade, discard some of the seeds from the large chilies.

A view of the Ayung river from the resort pool—Sayan

Singapore chili crab

3–4 lb (1 1/2–2 kg) live crabs
Vegetable oil for deep-frying
6–7 shallots, very finely chopped
8–10 cloves garlic, very finely chopped
3 tablespoons very finely chopped fresh
  ginger
4 bird's-eye chilies, chopped
3 1/2 cups (875 ml) chicken stock
3–4 tablespoons hot bean paste
1/4 cup (60 ml) bottled chili sauce
1/2 cup (125 ml) tomato sauce
1 tablespoon sugar
2 1/2 tablespoons Chinese rice wine
  (preferably Shao Hsing)
2 teaspoons salt
1 teaspoon white pepper
2 eggs, lightly beaten
2 tablespoons potato starch or cornstarch, mixed with 3 tablespoons
  water
1 scallion (spring onion), cut in 2-in
  (5-cm) lengths
French bread or other bread for serving

Chili-ginger sauce
1/2 teaspoon salt
6 large red chilies, chopped
5–6 cloves garlic
2 tablespoons finely chopped fresh
  ginger
2 teaspoons sugar
1 teaspoon rice vinegar
1 teaspoon water

One of the all-time great seafood dishes of tropical Asia, Singapore chili crab is an irresistible feast of succulent meaty crabs dripping with a hot spicy sauce, which is thickened with beaten egg and corn-starch. It is best enjoyed with chunks of French bread for soaking up the rich sauce. Don't forget to serve with finger bowls as this is a hands-on dish!

1 Stun the crabs by putting them in the freezer for 15–20 minutes. Cut in half lengthways with a cleaver and remove the backs and spongy crab matter. Remove claws from the body and crack with a cleaver in several places. Cut each body half into 2–3 pieces, leaving legs attached. Wash (scrub with a soft brush if necessary), drain thoroughly, and pat completely dry.
2 Heat the oil in a wok until very hot. Have the wok cover or a large lid handy to hold over the wok. Add the crab pieces, a few at a time, and deep-fry 2 minutes, holding the lid above the oil as it will splutter. Drain crab pieces well and set aside. Remove all but 2 tablespoons oil from the wok.
3 Prepare chili-ginger sauce by blending all ingredients to a smooth paste. Set aside. Reheat oil and add shallots, garlic, ginger, and chilies. Stir-fry over low–medium heat until fragrant, about 3 minutes, then add chicken stock, hot bean paste, chili-ginger sauce, chili sauce, tomato sauce, sugar, rice wine, salt, and pepper. Bring to a boil, lower heat, and simmer 2 minutes. Add the crab pieces and simmer until cooked, 3–4 minutes.
4 Stir in the potato starch or cornstarch mixed with water, stirring until the sauce thickens and clears. Add the eggs and stir until set, then transfer the chili crab to a serving dish. Garnish with scallion and serve with crusty French bread.

Note: Hot bean paste is made with fermented soy beans, *tau cheong*, which is sometimes labelled "salted soya beans" or "yellow bean sauce," with additional chili and seasonings. If you cannot obtain hot bean paste, use regular salted soybean paste and add another 2 bird's-eye chilies.

Presidential suite—Four Seasons Hotel Singapore

Sumatran chicken laksa

2 tablespoons vegetable oil
3 cups (750 ml) coconut milk
3 cups (750 ml) chicken stock
13 oz (400 g) chicken breast or thigh
 fillet, shredded
Salt and black pepper to taste
13 oz (400 g) fresh or 6 1/2 oz (200 g)
 dried rice ribbon noodles, cooked in
 boiling water, drained
1 1/2 cups (100 g) loosely packed bean
 sprouts, straggly tails discarded
2 hard-boiled eggs, sliced
6 1/2 oz (200 g) firm tofu, fried, sliced
2 tablespoons chopped fresh cilantro
 (coriander) leaves
2 tablespoons chopped scallion (spring
 onion)
1 medium red chili, finely julienned
1 lime or lemon, quartered
Chili *sambal* (see Note)

Laksa paste
2 tablespoons small dried shrimp,
 soaked in hot water to soften, drained
8 shallots, chopped
4–5 cloves garlic, chopped
2 tablespoons finely chopped galangal
2 tablespoons finely chopped fresh
 turmeric
6 candlenuts, chopped
5–6 large red chilies, sliced
2 stems lemongrass, sliced
1 1/2 teaspoons dried shrimp paste
3 teaspoons fish sauce
1/2 cup (125 ml) coconut cream

Laksa, a noodle soup with spicy coconut-milk broth and rice-flour noodles, is popular in Malaysia, Singapore, and Indonesia. Chicken, bean sprouts, tofu, and boiled eggs enrich this satisfying Sumatran version, which relies on freshly made laksa paste for maximum flavor.

1 To prepare the laksa paste, process the dried shrimp until finely shredded. Add all the remaining ingredients except coconut cream and process until coarsely ground. Add the coconut cream and process to a smooth paste. Set aside.
2 Heat the oil in a large saucepan and add laksa paste. Then stir-fry over low-medium heat until fragrant, 4–5 minutes. Slowly add the coconut milk, stirring, then add the chicken stock. Bring to a boil, lower heat and simmer uncovered, 10 minutes.
3 Add chicken and simmer until just cooked. Taste and add salt and freshly ground black pepper to taste.
4 To serve, divide the noodles between 4 large bowls. Top with chicken soup and garnish each serving with some of the bean sprouts, egg slices, tofu, cilantro, and scallion. Serve with lime wedges and chili *sambal* for adding to taste.

Note: To reduce the richness of the soup, the coconut cream in the laksa paste could be reduced to 1/4 cup (60 ml). To make a quick chili *sambal* to accompany this dish, pound or process 6 seeded and chopped large red chilies together with 1 teaspoon toasted dried shrimp paste to form a smooth paste. Divide between 4 small bowls and add a small green lime to each for squeezing into the *sambal* to taste.

Resort Chef Vindex Valentino—Four Seasons Resort Sayan

Nasi campur

Coconut rice
4 cloves garlic, crushed
1 pandan leaf, raked with a fork
  and tied in a knot
1 kaffir lime leaf, edges torn
1 *salam* leaf (optional)
1/2 teaspoon salt
1 cup (250 ml) coconut milk
1 1/2 cups (375 ml) water
2 cups (400 g) long-grain rice, washed
  and drained

Braised *rendang* beef
4 shallots, chopped
4–5 cloves garlic, chopped
2 teaspoons finely chopped fresh ginger
2 teaspoons finely chopped turmeric
1 teaspoon finely chopped galangal
6–8 large red chilies, seeds discarded,
  chopped
4–5 bird's-eye chilies, sliced
4 candlenuts, dry roasted and chopped
3 tablespoons vegetable oil
2 teaspoons coriander powder
1 teaspoon cumin powder
2 kaffir lime leaves
2 *salam* leaf (optional)
3 stems lemongrass, bruised and
  each cut into 3 pieces
2 1/2 cups (300 g) coconut milk
1/2 cup (50 g) freshly grated or
  desiccated coconut, toasted in a dry
  wok until golden brown
8 oz (250 g) beef tenderloin, cut in
  2-cm (1-in) cubes
Salt to taste
Freshly ground black pepper to taste

Chicken with sweet soy and chili sauce
1/4 cup (60 ml) sweet soy sauce (*kecap
  manis*)
1/4 cup (60 ml) light soy sauce
2 teaspoons oyster sauce
1 teaspoon sesame oil
2 tablespoons vegetable oil
2 shallots, thinly sliced
2 cloves garlic, finely chopped
1 tablespoon thinly sliced leek, or white
  part of scallion (spring onion)
2 large red chilies, sliced
13 oz (400 g) chicken breast, cut in
  3/4-in (1 1/2 cm) dice
White pepper to taste

Crackers with crispy eggs
8 dried crackers (*krupuk*)
Oil for deep frying
4 hard-boiled eggs, peeled

This version of *nasi campur* (literally "mixed rice") is like a mini-Rijstaffel with pandan-flavored coconut rice; *rendang*-style beef; chicken stir-fried with soy and chili sauce; crackers with crispy hard-boiled eggs; a Balinese-style vegetable mix (page 185); pickled cucumber (page 185); crispy *tempe* (page 185) and two fresh *sambal* (page 185). As several of the components can be prepared well in advance, this recipe is not as complex as it may seem. And you can prepare any of these recipes individually to serve with plain rice and other dishes.

Coconut rice
1 Put all ingredients except rice in a saucepan with a heavy base and bring slowly to a boil, stirring frequently.
2 Add the rice, stir, then partially cover the pan with a lid. Cook over moderate heat until the coconut milk is completely absorbed and "craters" form on the surface, about 5 minutes. Cover the pan firmly, turn off heat, and stand 5 minutes. Wipe the inside of the lid with a towel, cover the pan firmly, and cook over very low heat, 15 minutes. Remove from the heat.
3 Remove pandan, lime, and *salam* leaves, and fluff up rice with a fork. Cover and stand at least 5 minutes, or up to 20 minutes before serving.

Braised *rendang* beef
1 Process shallots, garlic, ginger, turmeric, galangal, chilies, and candlenuts to a smooth paste, adding a little of the oil if needed to keep the mixture turning.
2 Heat oil in a small saucepan and stir-fry the paste over low–moderate heat until fragrant, about 3 minutes. Add the coriander and cumin powders, lime and *salam* leaves, and lemongrass and continue stir-frying until the ingredients are cooked, 4–5 minutes. Process toasted coconut to an oily paste and add to the pan along with the coconut milk. Bring slowly to a boil, stirring constantly.
3 Add the beef and cook, uncovered, over moderate heat, stirring frequently, until the beef is tender and the sauce has almost dried up, 30–45 minutes. Add a little water if the sauce dries up before the meat is cooked. Season with salt and pepper to taste.

Chicken with sweet soy and chili sauce
1 Combine both lots of soy sauce, oyster sauce, and sesame oil in a small bowl and set aside.
2 Heat vegetable oil in a wok and add shallots, garlic, leek, and chilies. Stir-fry over high heat, 30 seconds, then add chicken and stir-fry 2 minutes. Add sauce mixture and continue stir-frying until the chicken is cooked, about 2 minutes. Sprinkle with pepper and serve hot.

Cackers with crispy eggs
1 Dry crackers in a sunny place for a day. Heat oil in a large pan and add a few crackers at a time. When they expand, remove with a slotted spoon and drain.
2 Deep-fry hard-boiled eggs until crisp and golden brown on the outside. Drain on paper towel, cut in half and serve with sweet *sambal* (page 185).

Tandoori lamb, chicken, or tiger prawns

4 small racks of lamb, or 4 skinless
  chicken breasts, or 12 tiger prawns,
  peeled and deveined, with final tail
  section left intact
2 tablespoons butter, melted

Marinade
1 cup (250 ml) thick plain yogurt
3 tablespoons cream
1 egg yolk
2 1/2 tablespoons finely chopped garlic
2 tablespoon finely chopped ginger
1 teaspoon salt
2 tablespoons lime or lemon juice
2 teaspoons ajowan (carom) seeds
  (if cooking prawns)
2 teaspoons *garam masala*
2 teaspoons chili powder
1 teaspoon freshly ground black pepper
1 teaspoon turmeric powder
2 teaspoons finely chopped fresh
  cilantro (coriander) leaves

Salad
1 cup (100 g) finely julienned carrot
1/2 cup (50 g) finely julienned beetroot
1/2 cup (50 g) finely julienned jicama
  (substitute with onion)
1/2 cup (40 g) finely julienned
  cucumber
1/2 cup (70 g) finely julienned seeded
  tomato (optional, see Note)
1 small onion, thinly sliced
2 tablespoons lime or lemon juice
1 teaspoon *chat masala*

Food baked in a *tandoor* or clay oven in India is usually marinated in a mixture of yogurt (which acts as a tenderizer), plenty of ginger, and garlic plus spices. This marinade for lamb, chicken, or tiger prawns is further enriched with cream and egg yolk, and the barbecued items served with a refreshing side-salad. If you prefer, the meat can be marinated for as long as 24 hours in advance.

1 To prepare the marinade, put the yogurt in bowl and stir in the cream and egg yolk. Process garlic, ginger, salt, and lime juice to a smooth paste in a spice grinder, then add to the yogurt. Stir in all other marinade ingredients.
2 If cooking lamb, remove the skin from the lamb racks and prick meat all over to allow marinade to penetrate. Rub meat all over with the marinade, cover and refrigerate at least 3 hours, or overnight if preferred. Cook lamb racks over charcoal, turning until golden brown on all sides and cooked, or roast in a 350°F (180°C, gas 4) oven for about 20 minutes for medium-rare lamb. When meat is cooked, brush all over with melted butter and return to barbecue or oven for another 2 minutes.
3 If cooking chicken breasts, rub the chicken with the marinade and then refrigerate for at least 1 hour. Cook chicken breasts over hot charcoal or under a hot gas or electric broiler (grill), about 6 minutes on each side.
4 If cooking tiger prawns, mix prawns with the marinade, cover and refrigerate for at least 3 hours or overnight. Cook prawns over very hot charcoal, turning until golden brown and cooked, or cook under a broiler (grill), about 4 minutes per side. When the prawns are almost cooked, brush all over with melted butter and cook for a further 1 minute on each side.
5 While the meat or prawns are cooking, combine all the salad ingredients in a bowl, tossing to mix well. Serve with the cooked lamb, chicken, or tiger prawns.

Note: To remove the seeds from the tomato for the salad, cut tomato in half across and gently squeeze with the tomato held cut-side down.

Baraabaru design detail—Four Seasons Resort Maldives

Grilled pork back ribs with pumpkin and fennel slaw

2 quarts (2 liters) court bouillon (see Note)
2 whole star anise
1/2 teaspoon five-spice powder
4 sides baby pork back ribs, each about 1 1/2 lb (750 g), or 4–5 lb (2–2 1/2 kg) meaty pork shoulder ribs

Barbecue sauce
2 tablespoons vegetable oil
2 medium onions, chopped
2 tablespooons very finely chopped garlic
13-oz (400-g) can tomatoes with juice, tomatoes chopped
1 1/4 cups (300 ml) white vinegar
4 tablespoons brown sugar
1 tablespoon salt
1 tablespoon freshly ground black pepper
1 tablespoon paprika
1 tablespoon chili powder
1 tablespoon molasses
1 tablespoon *hoisin* sauce
1/2 cup (125 ml) orange juice
2 tablespoons English mustard powder

Lime chili dessing
2 tablespoons water
4 teaspoons sugar
2 tablespoons fish sauce
3 tablespoons lime juice
2 stems lemongrass, very finely chopped
1 kaffir lime leaf, very finely shredded
2–3 shallots, very finely chopped
1 red bird's-eye chili, finely chopped
2 teaspoons finely chopped mint
2 teaspoons finely chopped cilantro (coriander) leaves

Fennel and pumpkin slaw
1 large red chili, seeds discarded, finely sliced
3/4 cup (80 g) finely shredded long white Chinese (napa) cabbage
3/4 cup (80 g) firmly packed finely julienned fennel
1/2 cup (80 g) firmly packed finely julienned pumpkin
1 scallion (spring onion), shredded

These succulent pork ribs are simmered in court bouillon with typical Chinese spices, then drenched with a richly flavored barbecue sauce before being barbecued. The unusual accompaniment of cabbage, fennel, and julienned pumpkin with a herbed lime and chili dressing provides perfect balance, with its fresh flavors and crisp texture. If you can't obtain racks of baby pork back ribs, use meaty pork shoulder ribs.

1 To make the barbecue sauce, heat the oil in a large pan and add onions. Stir-fry over moderate heat until golden brown, then add all other sauce ingredients. Bring to a boil, stirring several times, then reduce heat and simmer uncovered over very low heat, 2 hours. Cool, then process to a purée.
2 While sauce is simmering, bring the court bouillon, star anise, and five-spice powder to a boil in a large saucepan. Cover and simmer 10 minutes, then add the pork ribs and simmer until tender, 1–1 1/2 hours. Drain and allow to cool.
3 Prepare the lime chili dressing. Put water and sugar in a small saucepan and bring to a boil, stirring. Simmer until the mixture thickens a little, then transfer to a bowl to cool. Stir in all other ingredients. Taste and add extra lime juice or fish sauce if required.
4 Just before serving, combine all the ingredients for fennel and pumpkin slaw in a bowl. Toss to mix, then add the lime chili dressing and toss again. Refrigerate while grilling the pork.
5 Put the pork ribs in a large bowl and pour over the barbecue sauce. Toss to coat the pork thoroughly, then grill over hot charcoal until fragrant and slightly charred. Serve accompanied by the fennel and pumpkin slaw.

Note: If you do not have time to make the barbecue sauce, use a commercial brand of sauce. If fresh or powdered court bouillon is not available, use light chicken stock with 1 teaspoon vinegar.

Fennel and pumpkin slaw

Vietnamese stir-fried beef tenderloin

1 lb (500 g) tenderloin or fillet steak,
    cut in 1-in (2 1/2-cm) cubes
Oil for deep-frying
Scant 1/4 cup (60 g) butter
1 large red onion, top and bottom
    trimmed, cut in 8–10 wedges
6–8 cloves garlic, thinly sliced
2 teaspoons coarsely crushed black
    pepper
2 scallions (spring onions), white part
    cut diagonally in 1 1/4-in (3-cm)
    lengths, green part finely julienned
1 tablespoon crisp-fried garlic slices,
    to garnish
1 *pappadum*, cut in any shape, to
    garnish

Marinade
2 stems lemongrass, very finely
    chopped
1/2 teaspoon chicken stock powder
1 teaspoon Chinese rice wine
1 teaspoon sugar
1 teaspoon black soy sauce
1 tablespoon potato starch or corn-
    starch
2 tablespoons water

Sauce
2 teaspoons fish sauce
2 teaspoons Maggi seasoning sauce
1 teaspoon Worchestershire sauce
1 teaspoon tomato sauce
1 teaspoon sugar
1/4 teaspoon sesame oil
1/4 cup (60 ml) chicken stock

These cubes of marinated beef have an excellent flavor and melting texture, thanks partly to the technique of blanching the beef in boiling oil before stir-frying it in butter with onion, garlic, and lashings of fragrant black pepper. Typical Vietnamese seasonings such as lemongrass and fish sauce join Western sauces to make a sophisticated yet easily prepared dish.

1 Put the beef cubes in a bowl. Sprinkle with all the marinade ingredients, then massage by hand until the liquid is absorbed. Refrigerate in a covered container for at least 2 hours.
2 Mix all the sauce ingredients together in a small bowl, stirring until the sugar dissolves, then set aside.
3 Pat the beef cubes dry with paper towel. Heat oil in a wok until smoking hot. Deep-fry the marinated beef cubes, a few at a time, for just 10 seconds. Remove with a slotted spoon and drain on paper towel.
4 Remove the oil from the wok and add butter. When it is hot, add the onion wedges, garlic, and white part of the scallions, and stir-fry over high heat, 30 seconds. Add the black pepper and stir-fry for about 15 seconds, then add the beef and the prepared sauce and stir-fry over high heat until the beef is just cooked, about 2 minutes. Serve immediately on a bed of scallion greens, and garnish with crisp-fried garlic slices and, if desired, *pappadum*.

Grilled beef with rendang marinade

4 thick pieces fillet steak, each about
  6 1/2 oz (200 g)
1/2 teaspoon salt
1/4 teaspoon freshly ground black
  pepper
1 tablespoon coriander powder
1 tablespoon pink peppercorns,
  crushed

Rendang spice paste
2 tablespoons vegetable oil
4 red or green bird's-eye chilies, finely
  chopped
1/2 in (1 cm) galangal, sliced
1/2 in (1 cm) fresh ginger, sliced
2 shallots, sliced
1 clove garlic, sliced
1 stem lemongrass, thinly sliced
2 candlenuts, chopped
1/2 teaspoon coriander powder
1/4 teaspoon cumin powder
1 *salam* leaf, torn (optional)
1 kaffir lime leaf, sliced
4 large red chilies, sliced
1/4 cup (60 ml) water

Rendang—a Sumatran specialty of beef cooked with chilies, aromatic roots, herbs, and spices—is the inspiration for this light, modern recipe. Instead of being simmered in coconut milk, the meat is briefly marinated in a typical *rendang* spice paste, then grilled to fragrant perfection.

1 To prepare the *rendang* spice paste, heat the oil in a small pan and add the bird's eye chilies, galangal, ginger, shallots, garlic, lemongrass, and candlenuts. Stir fry over low heat, 4–5 minutes. Add the coriander and cumin powders, *salam* leaf (if using) and kaffir lime leaf. Stir-fry for 1 minute, then remove from the heat. Remove *salam* leaf but do not discard.
2 Process the spice paste ingredients until smooth. Return the spice paste and *salam* leaf to the pan and add the finely chopped red chilies. Rinse out the blender with the water and add to the pan. Cook the spice paste over low heat, stirring frequently, until the paste is cooked and thick, about 10 minutes; add a little more water from time to time if the paste threatens to stick. Cool and discard *salam* leaf.
3 Season the beef with salt, black pepper, coriander powder, and pink peppercorns. Smear both sides of the meat with the spice paste and set aside to marinate for about 15 minutes. Grill over high heat until done to taste. Serve on a bed of leaves for visual effect, if desired.

Panoramic view from Jati Bar—Four Seasons Resort Sayan

Coriander-marinated beef sirloin with fragrant sauce

1/4 cup (60 ml) light soy sauce
1/3 cup (60 ml) water
1 tablespoon sugar
2 teaspoons coriander seeds, toasted
  and coarsely crushed (see Note)
3–4 cloves garlic, smashed and finely
  chopped
4 sirloin or fillet steaks, each about 6 oz
  (180 g), fat trimmed and discarded
2 teaspoons vegetable oil
Sprigs of land cress or watercress to
  garnish

Fragrant sauce
1 1/2 tablespoons vegetable oil
5–6 shallots, chopped
4–5 cloves garlic, chopped
2 large red chilies, chopped
1 red or green bird's-eye chili, chopped
2 teaspoons finely chopped galangal
2 teaspoons finely chopped fresh ginger
1 cup (250 ml) chicken stock
1 teaspoon coriander powder
4 cloves
1/4 teaspoon freshly grated nutmeg
1/3 cup (85 ml) sweet soy sauce (*kecap
  manis*)
4 teaspoons light soy sauce
Salt and pepper to taste

Semur, a Dutch-inspired dish of braised beef simmered in a sauce accented with soy sauce, coriander, and freshly grated nutmeg, is given a modern twist in this recipe. Sirloin steaks are used instead of stewing beef, with some of the traditional seasonings used in the marinade, while others appear in the accompanying sauce. This truly delicious sauce—which is so good you'll never eat steak any other way—can be prepared in advance to save time.

1 To prepare the fragrant sauce, heat oil in a small pan and add the shallots, garlic, chilies, galangal, and ginger. Stir-fry over low heat for 10 minutes. Add 1/2 cup (125 ml) of the stock and the coriander powder and cloves. Bring to a boil and simmer 2–3 minutes. Cool, then process in a blender until smooth. Return to the saucepan, add remaining chicken stock, nutmeg, and sweet soy sauce. Cover and simmer for 15 minutes. Taste the sauce and add salt and pepper if desired.
2 While sauce is simmering, combine soy sauce, water, sugar, coriander seeds, and garlic in a bowl, stirring to mix well. Add the steak and set aside to marinade for about 25 minutes, turning the steak a couple of times.
3 Heat oil in a non-stick or cast-iron pan until very hot. Add the steaks and sear on both sides. Lower heat slightly and cook to taste. Pour over the sauce, stir for a few seconds to heat through, then transfer beef to a serving dish. Garnish with cress.

Note: Do not used finely ground coriander for the beef marinade; whole spice seeds lightly toasted and coarsely crushed give a superior flavor and texture.

Ayung Terrace—Four Seasons Resort Bali at Sayan

Upside-down fruit cakes

1–2 teaspoons superfine (caster) sugar
  for sprinkling on tart tins
3/4 cup (85 g) finely ground almonds
  (almond meal)
1/3 cup (85 g) superfine (caster) sugar
2 large eggs
1/4 cup (30 g) all-purpose (plain) flour
1/3 teaspoon baking powder
1/4 cup (50 g) butter, melted

Topping
1 tablespoon soft brown or Demerara
  sugar
1 tablespoon butter
4 small slices fresh mango
4 small thin wedges pineapple, or
  2 small apricots, halved
4 small pieces papaya, or 2 small ripe
  plums, halved
8 slices of banana, or 8 cherries, stoned
1–2 teaspoons superfine (caster) sugar

Upside-down tarts or cakes are always delicious, and especially so if the fruit used is a luscious tropical fruit such as mango, pineapple, papaya, and banana. Other tropical fruits that would be perfect for this dish are guava, pineapple, and sapodilla (*ciku*). Even if you can obtain only temperate climate fruit, you can still make this recipe, which has a rich almond topping. Served warm with whipped cream, this impressive dessert is ideal for a special occasion.

1 To prepare the topping, put brown sugar and butter in a saucepan and melt, stirring. Add the fruit and sauté on all sides over moderate heat, 1 1/2 minutes.
2 Grease the inside of 4 small tart tins or heat-proof dishes, each 3 in (8 cm) in diameter and at least 2 in (5 cm) high. Sprinkle the greased part with 1–2 teaspoons sugar, then divide the fruit evenly between the tins or dish.
3 Put the almonds, sugar, and eggs in a food processor and mix at high speed until sponge-like. Add the flour and baking powder, processing at low speed to mix, then pour in the melted butter.
4 Pour the cake mixture over the top of the fruit in each dish, and bake at 350°F (180°C, gas 4) until done, 25–30 minutes. (A skewer inserted into the cake should come out dry.) Allow to cool slightly, then unmold by running a knife around the inside of each dish and turning it upside-down onto a serving plate, so the fruit is facing up. Serve warm with whipped cream.

Note: To make one large upside-down fruit cake for about 8 people, double the proportion of all the ingredients and use a round cake tin 6 1/2 in (16 cm) in diameter with sides abut 2 in (5 cm) tall. Bake at 340°F (175°C, gas 3 3/4) for about 35–40 minutes.

Baked coconut cream custard

2 cups (500 ml) light (single) cream
1/2 cup (125 ml) coconut cream
1/4 cup (60 g) sugar
6 egg yolks
2 tablespoons coconut liqueur (such as
  Malibu)
Fresh mint leaves, to garnish

The rich, creamy taste of coconut permeates countless tropical dishes, from soups and curries to desserts. In this variation of the classic baked custard, coconut cream is combined with regular dairy cream, sugar, and egg yolks, with a dash of coconut liqueur adding even more flavor and fragrance to make a very special dessert.

1 Preheat oven to 350°F (180°C, gas 4).
2 Put the cream and coconut cream in a saucepan and heat slowly, stirring constantly. Do not allow to come to a boil. Remove from the heat.
3 Beat the sugar and egg yolks together until the sugar is dissolved and the yolks frothy. Pour in the hot cream slowly, stirring constantly. Pour the mixture slowly back into the saucepan and cook over low heat, stirring constantly, for just 1 minute.
4 Strain the mixture into a bowl and stir in the coconut liqueur. Transfer the mixture to 4 individual ramekins and set them in a baking dish of warm water. Cook in preheated oven until the custards are set, 30–40 minutes. Cool the custards then sprinkle 1 teaspoon sugar on the top of each custard and brown under a broiler (grill) to form a glaze. Serve warm or chilled. Garnish with a few fresh mint leaves, if desired.

Note: If you do not have coconut liqueur, you could add 2 tablespoons white rum and a few drops of coconut essence. For a lighter version of this recipe, substitute 1 cup (250 ml) of the cream with 1 cup (250 ml) milk. Alternatively, use 1 3/4 cup (450 ml) milk and 3/4 cup (175 ml) coconut cream.

Tropical hideaways—Four Seasons Resorts Bali

Pineapple crumble

1 small ripe pineapple, about 1 1/2–2 lb
   (800 g–1 kg), peeled, quartered
   lengthways, cores reserved
1 tablespoon butter
4 tablespoons sugar
1 vanilla bean
1 tablespoon lemon juice
2 teaspoons brown rum
2 teaspoons pineapple liqueur, or
   additional 1 teaspoon rum
1 teaspoons cornstarch, mixed with
   2 teaspoons water

Crumble topping
1 1/4 cup (150 g) all-purpose (plain)
   flour
1/3–1/2 cup (85–125 g) sugar (depends
   on the seetness of the pineapple)
1/4 teaspoon vanilla essence
1/2 vanilla bean, split, seeds removed
1/4 cup (60 g) chilled butter, cut in
   fine dice

The popular apple crumble of temperate regions takes on a whole new meaning in the tropics when it's made with fresh pineapple flavored with rum and vanilla bean. Prepare the pineapple and the crumble topping in advance and refrigerate separately, then assemble and do the final cooking just before the meal for a trouble-free dessert.

1 Weigh the diced pineapple and keep 1 lb (500 g) for the crumble. Process the remainder together with the chopped core to obtain the juice; reserve 1/4 cup (60 ml) juice and keep any left over for another purpose.
2 Heat butter in a large saucepan and add the 1 lb (500 g) diced pineapple, 3 tablespoons of the sugar and the vanilla bean. Stir-fry over medium heat, 5 minutes. Transfer to a bowl. Put reserved pineapple juice, remaining 1 tablespoon sugar, lemon juice, rum, and cornstarch mixture in a small pan and cook over low heat, stirring constantly until the mixture thickens and clears. Add to the cooked pineapple, stirring to mix well.
3 To make the crumble topping, put flour, sugar (according to the sweetness of the pineapple), both lots of vanilla and butter in a food processor and pulse until the mixture resembles breadcrumbs; do not over-mix. Transfer to a bowl.
4 Preheat oven to 350°F (180°C, gas 4). Divide the pineapple mixture between 1 large or 4 small oven-proof bowls, discarding the vanilla bean. Sprinkle the pineapple with the prepared topping and bake in preheated oven until golden brown on top, 30–40 minutes. Serve warm with honey yogurt ice cream.

Honey yogurt ice cream

3/4 cup (185 ml) milk
3/4 cup (185 ml) light (single) cream
3 tablespoons honey
1/2 cup (125 g) superfine (caster) sugar
4 egg yolks
2 cups (500 ml) plain yogurt
1 teaspoon lemon juice

This delightfully fresh ice cream can be served with pineapple crumble or enjoyed with some almond biscotti or rolled coconut-milk wafers known as "love letters."

1 Put milk, cream, and honey into a saucepan and bring slowly almost to boiling point, stirring constantly. Remove from the heat.
2 Beat sugar and egg yolks together in a bowl until foamy, then slowly pour in a little of the milk mixture, stirring all the time. Return this to the milk mixture in the pan, return to the stove and cook over low heat, stirring constantly, until the mixture thickens slightly, about 3 minutes. Transfer to a bowl, cool, then refrigerate 30 minutes. Stir in the yogurt and lemon juice, then freeze in an ice cream maker. Transfer to a covered container and keep in the freezer until required.
3 Alternatively, transfer the mixture to a metal cake tin, cover with aluminum foil and freeze until icy around the edges, about 1 1/2 hours. Transfer to a food processor and blend to break up. Return the mixture to the tin, cover and freeze until firm, about 2 hours.
4 Transfer from the freezer to the refrigerator about 30 minutes before serving to soften slightly.

tropical party

It's party time! Celebrate outdoors, with plenty of oil lamps or scented candles. Even if you can't have a live *gamelan* orchestra gently playing its gongs and drums to set the mood, a CD of Asian music will do the trick. Finger-food is the name of the game when it comes to casual entertaining. Easy to eat, even easier to enjoy, you and your guests are going to love the results. Be sure to set out plenty of napkins and finger bowls; drop a slice of lime or lemon and an orchid flower in each, and the stage is set. The Vietnamese are renowned for their fresh rice-papers wrapped around a filling of bean sprouts, shredded vegetables, and noodles, or try them with a tuna filling, or even shrimp and chicken. Still using the idea of food in wrappers, our chefs from Bali suggest a curried vegetable filling inside whole-wheat *chapati*, as well as *naan* pockets stuffed with grilled meat and fresh herbs. An Indonesian variation on the same theme is pockets of pita bread filled with *rendang*-style beef, grilled chicken breast, or lamb marinated with lemongrass. Satay, skewers of seasoned meat, poultry, and shrimps with a peanut sauce, are popular in much of tropical Asia (and indeed, around the world). Heat the barbecue ready for delicious satay, accompanied by a rich peanut dipping sauce and pineapple *sambal*. Vegetarians will love the vegetable and tofu brochettes served with a cinnamon-soy sauce. Japanese *sushi* lends itself it all kinds of variations, and ours from Bali are entirely new. There's spicy chicken with mango, prawns atop a lemongrass *sambal*, regular *sushi* rice mixed with red "hill" rice with a crispy sweet *tempe* filling, and a *nori* roll of mixed vegetables. Other great party food is tropical pizza topped by stir-fried lamb with Chinese seasonings, chunks of tuna coated with sesame seeds, fragrant crab cakes with sweet chili dressing, delicious spicy snapper fillets wrapped and grilled in banana leaf, and a vegetarian version of Chinese pot-sticker dumplings that substitute eggplant for pork. Dessert as finger food? Have you ever thought of banana, chocolate, and fresh mint *samosa*? Our chef from the Maldives has, and offers you his creation.

Vietnamese summer rolls

4 large rice papers (9–12 in or 22–30 cm in diameter), or 12 small rice papers (about 6 1/2 in or 16 cm)
1 cup (100 g) finely julienned carrot, blanched in boiling water 1 minute, drained
1 cup (100 g) finely julienned jicama (yam bean) or long white radish (*daikon*)
3/4 cup (75 g) finely julienned cucumber
1/2 cup (50 g) finely julienned beetroot
1/2 avocado, cut in thin slices
2 dried black mushrooms, soaked in hot water to soften, stems discarded, caps finely shredded
1 1/4 oz (40 g) transparent mung bean noodles, soaked in warm water to soften, drained and cut in 2-in (5-cm) lengths
1/2 cup (20 g) loosely packed mint leaves
1/2 cup (20 g) loosely packed fresh cilantro (coriander) leaves
1 scallion (spring onion), cut in 1/2-in (1-cm) lengths
1 large red chili, seeds discarded, very finely shredded lengthways

Pickled bean sprouts
1/2 cup (125 ml) water
1/4 cup (60 ml) white vinegar
1/4 cup (60 g) sugar
1/2 teaspoon salt
1 1/2 cups (100 g) loosely packed bean sprouts, straggly tails discarded

Ginger fish sauce dip
2 tablespoons water
1 tablespoon fish sauce
1 tablespoon lime or lemon juice
1 tablespoon very finely chopped garlic
1 tablespoon very finely chopped red chili
1 tablespoon very finely chopped fresh ginger

Tamarind avocado dip
1/2 avocado
1 tablespoon tamarind pulp, soaked in 1/4 cup (60 ml) warm water, squeezed and strained to obtain juice
1/4 cup (60 ml) white vinegar
1/4 cup (60 ml) fish sauce
1/4 cup (60 ml) grapeseed or vegetable oil
2 1/2 teaspoons sugar
2 1/2 teaspoons honey
1 large red chili, chopped
1 small clove garlic, chopped

Don't be intimidated by the long list of ingredients in this recipe. To save preparation time, make just one of the dips. However, when you have time to prepare this dish for a special occasion, it is well worth making all three dips. The tangy accompaniments to these fresh-flavored vegetable and herb rolls can be prepared well in advance. Shortly before serving, prepare the vegetables and wrap them in softened rice paper rolls.

1 To prepare the pickled bean sprouts, put the water, vinegar, sugar, and salt in a small saucepan and bring to a boil, stirring to dissolve the sugar. Allow to cool, then pour over the bean sprouts. Refrigerate for 1 hour before serving.
2 To make the ginger fish sauce dip, combine all ingredients in a bowl, stirring to mix well. Transfer to a sauce bowl and set aside.
3 To prepare the fragrant *sambal*, heat the oil in a small pan and add the shallots and garlic. Stir-fry over low heat for 2 minutes, then add all the remaining ingredients. Cook over low-medium heat, stirring frequently, for 8 minutes. Process in a spice grinder until smooth. Transfer to a sauce bowl and set aside.
4 Prepare tamarind avocado dip by processing all ingredients to make a smooth paste. Transfer to a sauce bowl and set aside.
5 Just before serving, arrange all the prepared vegetables and herbs on a table or bench. Dip a rice paper in a bowl of warm water for a few seconds until it starts to soften. Remove and place on a kitchen towel. Smooth the rice paper with your fingers. Repeat with a second rice paper.
6 Neatly arrange one-quarter of each of the vegetables, noodles, and herbs side-by-side across the center of a rice paper, to within 3/4 in (2 cm) of each side. Roll up the rice paper, tucking in the edges to make a cigar shape and completely enclose the filling. Repeat with the remaining rice papers. Cut each roll diagonally in 5 bite-sized portions (3 if using small rice papers) and transfer to a serving plate. Add one-quarter of the pickled bean sprouts and sprinkle over some of the shredded red chili. Serve with the prepared dips and *sambal* in separate sauce bowls.

Fragrant *sambal*
2 tablespoons vegetable oil
3 shallots, finely chopped
1 clove garlic, finely chopped
2 large red chilies, seeds discarded, chopped
1 teaspoon very finely chopped galangal
1 teaspoon very finely chopped fresh ginger
1/4 large tomato, chopped
1 tablespoon sweet soy sauce (*kecap manis*)
1 teaspoon sugar
1 teaspoon lime juice
1/2 teaspoon salt
Pinch freshly ground black pepper

Vegetable and tofu brochettes with cinnamon-soy sauce

8 bamboo satay skewers
1 medium zucchini (courgette), cut in 8 slices, each 3/4-in (2-cm) thick, blanched in boiling water, 2 minutes
1 large red or green bell pepper (capsicum), cut in 8 pieces, each about 3/4-in (2-cm) square, blanched in boiling water, 2 minutes
1 large onion, blanched in boiling water, 2 minutes, then cut in 8 wedges
8 small button mushrooms, stems discarded
1–2 cakes firm tofu, cut in 8 pieces about 3/4-in (2-cm) square, deep-fried until golden brown
2 tablespoons coriander seeds, lightly toasted, very coarsely crushed

Cinnamon-soy sauce
3 tablespoons vegetable oil
3–4 shallots, chopped
2 cloves garlic, chopped
1 teaspoon very finely chopped galangal
1 teaspoon very fresh ginger
1 large red chili, chopped
1 red or green bird's-eye chili, chopped
1/2 cup (125 ml) vegetable or chicken stock
3 tablespoons sweet soy sauce (*kecap manis*)
1/2 teaspoon salt
1/2 teaspoon coriander powder
1/2 teaspoon cinnamon powder
1/2 teaspoon freshly grated nutmeg
1/2 teaspoon white pepper
1/8 teaspoon ground cloves
Salt to taste

These skewers of zucchini, bell pepper, onion, mushroom, and tofu are ideal for vegetarians, and are equally good served with barbecued meat or poultry. The basting sauce is accented with aromatics and warm spices including cinnamon, coriander, nutmeg, and cloves for a truly tropical flavor.

1 To prepare the cinnamon-soy sauce, heat the oil in a small saucepan and add shallots, garlic, galangal, ginger, and both lots of chili. Stir-fry over low heat until softened and fragrant, 4–5 minutes. Add all other ingredients. Bring to a boil, reduce heat and simmer until the sauce reduces by about one-half, 8–10 minutes. Cool, then transfer to a blender and process to a smooth paste. Transfer sauce to a wide bowl.
2 Thread 1 piece each of zucchini, bell pepper, onion, mushroom, and tofu onto each skewer. Paint the skewers with the cinnamon-soy sauce, covering all over. Sprinkle each skewer with coriander seeds and grill over a moderately hot fire, turning several times, until cooked.

Note: Do not grind the coriander seeds finely. Pound with a pestle or pulse a few times in a spice grinder. Alternatively, put toasted seeds in a small plastic bag and roll with a rolling pin.

Chapati vegetable wrap with pineapple and cucumber raita

2 tablespoons vegetable oil
1 small white onion, finely chopped
1 small carrot, julienned
1 very small zucchini (courgette), julienned
1 very small eggplant (aubergine),
  julienned
1/4 red plus 1/4 yellow bell pepper
  (capsicum), julienned
1–2 teaspoons Madras curry powder
1 tablespoon plain yogurt
1/2 teaspoon salt
Freshly ground black pepper to taste
4 wholemeal *chapati* or large *tortilla*
Sprigs of fresh cilantro (coriander)
  leaves to garnish

Curry sauce
6 shallots, finely chopped
4 cloves garlic, finely chopped
1 teaspoon finely chopped fresh ginger
1 teaspoon finely chopped galangal
1 teaspoon finely chopped turmeric
2 candlenuts, chopped
1 1/2 tablespoon vegetable oil
1/2 teaspoon salt
2 kaffir lime leaves
1 teaspoon coriander powder
1 tablespoon Madras curry powder
3/4 cup (185 ml) coconut milk

Pineapple and cucumber *raita*
3/4 cup (185 ml) plain yogurt
1/4 teaspoon salt
Liberal sprinkling white pepper
3/4 teaspoon cumin powder
1/2 cup (65 g) finely diced cucumber
1/2 cup (65 g) finely diced pineapple

Wholemeal unleavened bread or *chapati* is normally dipped in curry gravy or lentils as part of a meal but in this creative recipe it's used as a wrap for a mixture of lightly stir-fried vegetables bathed in a fragrant curry gravy. The fresh tang of pineapple and cucumber in yogurt makes an ideal accompaniment.

1 Prepare the pineapple and cucumber *raita* first. Combine yogurt, salt, pepper, and cumin powder in a bowl, stirring to mix well. Add cucumber and pineapple and chill for at least 30 minutes.
2 To make the curry sauce, process shallots, garlic, ginger, galangal, turmeric, and candlenuts to a paste in a spice grinder, adding a little of the oil if needed. Heat oil in a small pan, add the ground mixture and stir-fry over low heat until fragrant, 3–4 minutes. Add all remaining ingredients and bring to a boil, stirring. Simmer uncovered for 10 minutes, then discard lime leaves. Set aside.
3 To finalize the dish, heat oil in a wok and add onion, carrot, zucchini, eggplant, and both lots of bell pepper. Stir-fry over moderate-high heat until cooked but not soft, 2–3 minutes. Sprinkle with curry powder, then stir in the prepared curry sauce. Remove from heat and stir in the yogurt, salt, and pepper. Set aside.
4 Reheat the *chapati* in a dry skillet or microwave, then transfer to a counter top. Arrange one-quarter of the vegetable and curry filling down the center of each *chapati*, then roll over to enclose filling. Serve garnished with cilantro sprigs and accompanied by the *raita*.

Note: To make *chapati*, sift 2 cups (230 g) wholemeal (*atta*) flour into a bowl with 1/2 teaspoon salt and 1 tablespoon clarified butter (*ghee*) or butter. Make a well in the center and add 2/3 cup (150 ml) water and 2 teaspoons oil. Mix well by hand to form a soft dough, knead for 10 minutes and rest 15 minutes. Divide into 6 portions, flatten each one in your palm by pressing with your finges. Roll one disc out into a thin pancake, 5 in (13 cm) in diameter. Cook on a dry, medium-hot skillet or griddle for 2 minutes. When bubbles start to appear, flip it over and cook until brown spots form underneath.

Barbecued curd cheese and vegetable stacks

1 cup (160 g) firm Indian curd cheese (*paneer*), or baked ricotta, cut into 8 cubes
1 medium green bell pepper (capsicum), cut in 8 pieces
1 medium onion, cut in 8 wedges
1 medium tomato, cut in 8 wedges
4 large or 8 small skewers
1/2 teaspoon *chat masala*
2 teaspoons finely chopped fresh cilantro (coriander) leaves
1 lime or lemon, quartered

Indian curd cheese
4 cups (1 liter) milk
1/4 cup (65 ml) lemon juice
2 cups (500 ml) iced water

White *tandoori masala*
2 teaspoons finely chopped ginger
2 teaspoons finely chopped garlic
1 1/2 teaspoons lime juice
1 tablespoon mustard or vegetable oil
2 teaspoons chick pea flour (*besan*)
1/2 cup (125 ml) thick natural yogurt
1/2 teaspoon *chat masala*
1/4 teaspoon cumin powder
1/8 teaspoon ajwan (*carom*) powder (optional)
1/4 teaspon mustard paste
Liberal sprinkling of white pepper

This is an elegant vegetarian dish, developed for cooking in the widely popular *tandoor* or clay oven of northwest India. It uses firm Indian curd cheese or *paneer* (which can be substituted with baked ricotta), together with vegetables, marinating them in a chili-free or "white" *tandoori* marinade. Although it doesn't generate the same heat, a barbecue or regular broiler (grill) is an ideal substitute for a *tandoor*.

1 If readymade Indian curd cheese (*paneer*) or baked ricotta are not available, make your own. Put the milk in a saucepan and heat slowly, stirring, until it almost comes to a boil. Remove from heat, add lemon juice and stir vigorously until it curdles. Add iced water, stir and pour into a sieve lined with cheesecloth. Tie ends of cheesecloth and leave to drain 1 1/2 hours. Squeeze the cheese gently while still inside the cheesecloth, then shape it to form a rectangle. Wrap the the cheesecloth in a thick towel. Put a flat board on top of the cheese, weighing it down with a several heavy cans of food. Leave for 4 hours in a cool place to become firm. Refrigerate in a covered container until required.
2 Prepare the white *tandoori masala*. Process ginger, garlic, and lime juice in a spice grinder to make a smooth paste. Set aside. Heat oil in a small saucepan and stir in chick pea flour. Stir over low heat for 1–2 minutes to make a paste. Add garlic and ginger paste and stir-fry for 30 seconds, then add all other ingredients and cook over low heat for 1 minute. Cooll before using.
3 Put the cheese cubes in a bowl. Add half the white *tandoori masala* to the cheese and toss gently to coat. Put the bell pepper, onion, and tomato in a separate bowl and toss with the remaining *masala*. Refrigerate both for 1 hour.
4 Divide the cheese cubes, bell pepper, onion, and tomato between the skewers. Cook over very hot charcoal or under a very hot grill, turning, until done, about 5 minutes. Serve on the skewer or remove from the skewers to a plate. Garnish with lime juice, *chat masala*, and chopped cilantro leaves.

Sunset—Four Seasons Resort Maldives

Potato samosa with tamarind sauce

2 cups (250 g) all-purpose (plain) flour,
  plus extra for kneading
2 tablespoons vegetable oil
1/2 cup (125 ml) water
Vegetable oil for deep-frying

Potato filling
2 tablespoons vegetable oil
2 teaspoons brown mustard seeds
1 medium onion, chopped
1–2 large green chilies, chopped
10–12 curry leaves, chopped
1 teaspoon turmeric
1/2 teaspoon very finely chopped garlic
1/2 teaspoon very finely chopped fresh
  ginger
11 oz (350 g) potatoes, boiled and
  mashed
5 oz (150 g) finely chopped carrots,
  blanched
1 tablespoon *chat masala*
1 teaspoon salt
2 tablespoons chopped fresh cilantro
  (coriander) leaves

Tamarind sauce
2 tablespoons tamarind pulp
1/2 cup (125 ml) warm water
3 1/2 tablespoons chopped mint leaves
2 cloves garlic
3 bird's-eye chilies
1 medium red chili
1/2 teaspoon salt
1/4 teaspoon sugar
1 tablespoon chopped fresh cilantro
  (coriander) leaves
1 scallion (spring onion), sliced

Samosa is a very popular savory snack in India, Maldives, Sri Lanka, and wherever Indian communities are found. A simple pastry of flour, oil, and water is used to enclose a spicy meat or vegetable filling—in this case, potato and carrot with herbs and spices, including the sour, salty, and inimitable *chat masala*. A tart tamarind sauce is the perfect dip for these savories.

1 To make the tamarind sauce, soak the tamarind in the water, squeeze, stir, and strain, discarding any solids. Grind mint, garlic, chilies, salt, and sugar in a mortar, then transfer to the tamarind water, stir, and garnish with cilantro and scallion.
2 For the potato filling, heat oil in a saucepan and add mustard seeds. Cook until they start to crackle, then add onion, chilies, and curry leaves and stir-fry over low-medium heat until onions turn golden. Add turmeric, garlic, and ginger and stir for 30 seconds, then add potatoes and stir to mix well. Transfer to a bowl and stir in the *chat masala*, salt, and cilantro. Set aside.
3 Put the flour in a bowl. Make a well in the center and pour in the oil and water. Stir to incorporate the liquid, then knead the dough on a floured board for about 10 minutes until soft but not sticky, adding a little extra flour if needed. Divide dough into balls, then flatten each with the hand. Roll out each disc of dough to a circle about 5 1/2 in (14 cm) in diameter. Cut each circle in half.
4 Put a heaped teaspoon of the filling on one side of each semi-circle. Moisten the top end of the dough with water, then fold over to enclose the filling, pressing the edges to seal firmly.
5 Heat oil in a wok until moderately hot. Deep-fry the *samosa*, a few at a time, until golden brown, 2–3 minutes. Drain on paper towel and serve hot or warm with the tamarind sauce.

Note: The potato filling, with the potato very roughly mashed before mixing with the seasonings, can be used as a vegetable dish.

Crispy stuffed tofu with chili and shallot dressing

2/3 cup (100 g) finely minced pork belly (see Note)
Scant 1 cup (100 g) crabmeat, flaked
1/4 teaspoon salt
Liberal pinch of white pepper
1 teaspoons finely chopped garlic
4 shallots, finely chopped
2 tablespoons chopped fresh cilantro (coriander) leaves
2 teaspoons oyster sauce
1 teaspoon sesame oil
1 teaspoon sugar
1 packet Japanese silken tofu (about 13 oz or 400 g), cut into 3 horizontal slices, drained on paper towel
4 egg whites, beaten until frothy but not stiff
1/2 cup (125 g) all-purpose (plain) flour
Vegetable oil for deep-frying
1/2 cup (125 ml) bottled Thai sweet chili sauce
1 teaspoon lime juice

Tofu is not only nutritious and fat-free, but is remarkably versatile. In this recipe, it is sandwiched with layers of seasoned minced pork and crabmeat for steaming. The cooked tofu is then dipped in flour and egg white and deep-fried for a meltingly smooth treat that is eaten with a quickly made chili sauce dip. Most of the preparation can be done in advance, making this ideal for entertaining.

1 Put pork, crabmeat, salt, pepper, garlic, half the shallot, half the cilantro, the oyster sauce, sesame oil, and sugar into a food processor and process to make a paste. Place one slice of tofu on a heat-proof plate. Spread one-third of the mixture on this slice of tofu, then place a second slice of tofu on top. Spread the second slice of tofu with the remaining mixture, then top with the third slice of tofu. Pat gently with the hands to make an even stack.
2 Transfer the plate of tofu into a steamer and set the steamer over a wok of boiling water. Steam over high heat, 15 minutes, then remove from the steamer, cool, then chill in the refrigerator for 30 minutes. Do not refrigerate too long or the tofu will not be hot inside after frying.
3 Cut the tofu into 4 pieces and coat each lightly with flour. Dip one piece into the egg white, turning carefully to coat all sides. Heat oil in a wok and when very hot, deep-fry the stuffed tofu until golden brown and crisp, about 2–3 minutes. Repeat with remaining pieces of stuffed tofu.
4 Add the remaining chopped shallots and cilantro to the 1/2 cup (125 ml) bottled chili sauce and lime juice and serve as a dipping sauce for the tofu.

Note: Belly pork is recommended because of its texture and fat content; if you cannot obtain this, used regular minced pork containing at least ten percent fat.

Eggplant pot-stickers with a sesame dip

1 slender Asian eggplant (aubergine), about 6 1/2 oz (200 g), halved lengthways
1 1/2 tablespoons olive oil
Salt to taste
Freshly ground black pepper
2 tablespoons finely chopped basil leaves
1 teaspoons finely chopped fresh cilantro (coriander) leaves
4 shallots, finely chopped
Pinch of chili powder (optional)
2 teaspoons cornstarch
12 fresh or defrosted *won ton* wrappers
2 tablespoons vegetable oil
1/3 cup (85 ml) water
Mixture of fresh herbs to garnish, such as fresh cilantro (coriander) sprigs, basil, chives, tarragon, or chervil

Sesame dip
1 egg yolk
1/2 teaspoon Dijon mustard
1 teaspoon very finely chopped fresh cilantro (coriander) leaves
4 teaspoons salad oil (such as safflower or canola)
1 teaspoon sesame oil
Large pinch of salt
Freshly ground black pepper to taste
1/2 medium red chili, finely chopped
1/2 medium green chili, finely chopped

Inspired by Chinese meat-filled dumplings, these vegetarian dumplings are equally delicious. And what's more, they're easier than the traditional version as you can use ready-made *won ton* wrappers rather than make your own dough. The eggplant filling is full of flavor, while the mayonnaise-like dip—with Asian flavors of sesame oil and fresh cilantro—is excellent. These pot-stickers are so good you may want to make a double portion.

1 Preheat oven to 350°F (180°C, gas 4).
2 To prepare the sesame dip, put egg yolk, mustard, and cilantro in a small bowl and whisk to mix. Add the salad oil, a few drops at a time, whisking constantly until the sauce thickens. Add sesame oil and whisk in, then season with salt and pepper to taste and garnish with chopped red and green chili; set aside.
3 Brush the top of each eggplant with a little of the olive oil and sprinkle over salt, pepper, and a little of the basil. Cook in preheated oven until soft, about 15 minutes. Cool, then remove flesh from eggplant, and chop very finely.
4 Heat remaining oil and stir-fry the shallots over low-medium heat until transparent, 2–3 minutes. Add to the eggplant, together with the remaining basil, the cilantro, and chili powder. Taste and add salt and pepper if desired.
5 Sprinkle a plate with cornstarch. Moisten the edges of a *won ton* wrapper with a finger dipped in water. Place the wrapper on a board, and put about 1 heaped teaspoon of the filling in the center of each *won ton* wrapper. Bring up the front and back, as well as both sides, and pinch together to seal. Place each sealed dumpling on the floured plate as you work.
6 Heat remaining olive oil in a large non-stick skillet. When hot, add the dumplings, bottom side facing down, and cook until golden brown underneath, about 2 minutes. Add the water, cover the pan and cook until the water has evaporated, about 2 minutes. Transfer to a serving dish and serve with the sesame dip. Garnish with fresh herbs.

An alfresco wedding banquet—Four Seasons Resort Sayan

Tempura oysters with chili sauce

6 1/2 oz (200 g) shrimp meat or fish, chopped and pounded or blended to a paste
10-oz (300-g) cake soft plain tofu
Salt and pepper to taste
1/2 teaspoon sugar, or to taste
Pinch of cornstarch
1/2 teaspoon sesame oil
1 2/3 oz (50 g) bacon, finely chopped, fried until done, drained
10 freshly shucked oysters (10 oz/300 g)
1/2 cup (60 g) tempura flour
1 lime, sliced, to garnish
Chopped fresh cilantro (coriander) leaves to garnish
Oil for deep-frying
Chili sauce (see Note)

1 Pass tofu through a fine sieve and add shrimp paste. Stir in salt, pepper, sugar, cornstarch, sesame oil, and fried bacon bits and mix well. Refrigerate for 2 hours before using.
2 Lightly blanch oysters until almost half-cooked and dry with paper towel. If using large oysters, coat each one with some of the tofu paste by rolling in a bowl of tofu paste to form a dumpling. If using smaller oysters, use a spoon to roll several oysters in the paste together to form one large dumpling.
3 Coat each oyster dumpling with a layer of tempura flour, then deep-fry until golden brown. Drain on paper towel, transfer to a plate or back into their shells and drizzle chili sauce. Garnish with lime slices and cilantro.

Note: To prepare the chili sauce, combine 1 tablespoon chili sauce, 2 table-spoons tomato ketchup, 2 tablespoons lime juice, 2 tablespoons mango juice, 1 tablespoon chopped fresh cilantro (coriander) leaves, 3 chopped cloves garlic (or juice), and 1 teaspoon chopped chili (optional). Stir well.

Grilled tiger prawns with pickled nutmeg mayonnaise

1 lb 3 oz (600 g) raw medium tiger prawns, peeled and deveined
1 teaspoon salt
Liberal sprinkling white pepper

Pickled nutmeg mayonnaise
Pinch of gelatin powder
1 1/2 teaspoons warm water
1 1/4 cups (300 ml) mayonnaise
2 teaspoons lemon juice
5 teaspoons condensed milk
3 1/2 oz (100 g) pickled nutmeg slices, 4 slices retained as garnish, the remainder finely chopped
1/2 teaspoon black sesame seeds

1 To make the pickled nutmeg mayonnaise, melt gelatin in warm water, then add to the mayonnaise together with the lemon juice and milk. Refrigerate in a covered container for at least 1 hour or up to 2 weeks before serving. When ready to serve, stir in chopped nutmeg and sesame seeds; set aside.
2 Toss the prawns well in salt and pepper. Cook over hot charcoal or under a broiler (grill) until done, about 2–3 minutes per side. Drain on paper towel, divide between 4 plates and garnish each serving with a slice of pickled nutmeg and a portion of mayonnaise. Serve immediately. Another excellent way to prepare this dish is to dust the prawns in tempura flour and very briefly deep-fry them until cooked.

Sesame-crusted tuna chunks with a wasabi mayonnaise dip

10 oz (300 g) fresh tuna, cut in
  1 1/4-in (3-cm) cubes
1 tablespoon red *miso* paste
6 1/2 oz (200 g) raw shrimps, peeled
  and deveined
2 egg whites
1 tablespoon cornstarch
2 teaspoons lime juice
1 teaspoon light soy sauce
1/2 teaspoon salt
Liberal sprinkling of white pepper
1 clove garlic, finely chopped
3/4 cup (120 g) black and white sesame
  seeds
Vegetable oil for deep-frying
5 oz (150 g) long beans, topped and
  tailed, blanched and drained, then
  rinsed in iced water and well-drained

Sesame soy dressing
1/4 cup (60 ml) salad oil (not olive oil)
1 tablespoon light soy sauce
2 teaspoons rice vinegar
2 teaspoons sugar
2 teaspoons sesame oil
1 teaspoon very finely chopped garlic
1 teaspoon very finely chopped fresh
  ginger
1 teaspoon very finely chopped red
  chili
1 teaspoon *mirin* or sweet sherry
Salt and freshly ground black pepper to
  taste

***Wasabi* mayonnaise dip**
1–2 teaspoons *wasabi* powder mixed
  with a little water to form a paste, or
  1–2 teaspoons *wasabi* paste
1/2 cup (125 ml) mayonnaise

The rich, almost meaty flavor of fresh tuna is best appreciated either raw or just cooked. In this recipe, the tuna is first coated in Japanese soybean or *miso* paste, covered with a lightly seasoned shrimp paste then coated with sesame seeds. Deep-fried until the outside is crunchy and golden and the inside still meltingly tender, the tuna cubes can be served with a side-salad of beans tossed in a sesame-soy dressing, or speared with toothpicks and enjoyed with a *wasabi* mayonnaise dip.

1 Make the sesame soy dressing by combining all ingredients except salt and pepper in a bowl, whisking to mix well. Taste and season as desired. Toss with cooked long beans and set aside.
2 Put the tuna cubes in a bowl and add *miso* paste. Mix well by hand to coat the tuna, then set aside.
3 Process the shrimps in a food processor until coarsely ground. Add egg whites, cornstarch, lime juice, soy sauce, garlic, salt and pepper and blend to make a smooth paste. Add to the tuna and toss to coat.
4 Put sesame seeds in a separate bowl. Use tongs to coat each piece of tuna on all sides with the sesame seeds, so that they form a crust. Refrigerate 30 minutes.
5 Prepare the *wasabi* mayonnaise dip by mixing the *wasabi* and mayonnaise.
6 Heat oil in a wok and deep-fry the tuna pieces over very high heat just until the sesame seeds turn golden brown, about 1–1 1/2 minutes. Drain on paper towel and serve with the tossed long beans, and the *wasabi* mayonnaise dip.

Note: *Miso* paste keeps many months if refrigerated. It may dry out after storing; if this happens, mix it with 1–2 teaspoons warm water before tossing with the tuna.

Chili shrimp cakes with Thai sweet chili sauce

1 lb (500 g) medium-sized raw shrimps,
   peeled, deveined
6 1/2 oz (200 g) boneless skinned white
   fish (snapper, grouper, bream), cubed
1 egg, lightly beaten
1–2 tablespoons red Thai curry paste
1 tablespoon very finely chopped
   Chinese keys (*krachai*, see Note) or
   cilantro (coriander) root
2 tablespoons fish sauce
1 teaspoon baking soda
2 teaspoons sugar
1/2 teaspoon salt
1/2 teaspoon white pepper
3 cloves garlic, very finely chopped
1 kaffir lime leaf, very finely shredded
1 long bean or 3 green beans, thinly
   sliced
Vegetable oil for deep-frying

Thai sweet chili sauce
1/3 cup (85 g) sugar
2 teaspoons white vinegar
1/4 cup (50 g) very finely diced cucumber
1 tablespoon chopped dry-roasted
   cashew nuts
1 kaffir lime leaf, very finely shredded
1 large red chili, very finely chopped

Deep-fried shrimp or fish cakes are always popular. Thai red curry paste (which can be bought readymade) and other typical Thai seasonings including fish sauce, kaffir lime, and garlic make the basic mixture of fish and shrimps really flavorful in this recipe, while the accompanying sauce adds a touch of sweetness and heat.

1 Prepare the sauce first. Put sugar and vinegar into a small pan and cook over low heat, stirring, until the sugar dissolves. Simmer until the mixture becomes a little thick, about 2 minutes. Transfer to a bowl and leave to cool. Add cucumber, cashew nuts, lime leaf, and chili to the sauce and stir to mix well. Set aside.
2 Pulse shrimps and fish in a food processor until finely blended. Transfer to a metal, glass, or ceramic bowl. Fill a larger bowl with ice and set the bowl containing the shrimp mixture on top. Stir in the egg, curry paste, Chinese keys, fish sauce, baking soda, sugar, salt, pepper, garlic, lime leaf, and beans, mixing well.
3 Wet your hands and shape about 2 tablespoons of the mixture into a ball, then flatten slightly to make a cake about 3/4-in (2-cm) thick. (The shrimp cakes will swell during frying because of the baking soda.)
4 Heat oil for deep-frying in a wok. When hot, cook the shrimp cakes, a few at a time, until golden brown on both sides and cooked, 3–4 minutes. Drain on paper towel and serve hot with the sauce.

Note: Chinese keys—resembling a bunch of yellowish brown fingers—are available in glass jars, often labelled "rhizome." It is a good idea, each time you buy fresh cilantro (coriander), to wash, dry, and finely chop the roots and store them in an airtight container in the freezer, ready for future use in countless Thai recipes.

A reception at the rooftop lotus pond—Four Seasons Sayan

Grilled fish tikka in pandan leaf

1 tablespoon finely chopped fresh
  ginger
1 tablespoon finely chopped garlic
1 teaspoon salt
1 tablespoon lime juice
2 teaspoons turmeric powder
1 teaspoon chili powder
1 lb 3 oz (600 g) skinned and boned
  jack fish, trevally, or Spanish mackerel,
  cut in 1 3/4-in (4-cm) cubes
1–2 tablespoons vegetable oil
Pandan leaves for wrapping fish
1 lime, cut in quarters

Jack fish and the related trevally are both popular fish in tropical Asian waters. Because of their compact flesh, they are ideal for this recipe of marinated grilled fish cubes, although you could also use Spanish mackerel. If you are not serving other substantial dishes, you may want to double the amounts given as the flavor is so good that the fish will disappear quickly!

1 Pound or process the ginger, garlic, and salt together to make a smooth paste, adding some of the lime juice if needed. Transfer to a bowl and stir in lime juice, and turmeric and chili powders. Add the fish cubes and toss to coat well. Cover and marinate in the refrigerator for 2–3 hours.
2 Brush the fish pieces with oil, loosely wrap in pandan leaves and cook over moderately hot charcoal or under a grill, turning, until golden brown, about 8 minutes. Test with the tip of a sharp knife to make sure the fish is white in the center.
3 Serve hot with lime quarters.

Catch of the day—Four Seasons Resort Maldives

Banana bud salad with shrimps and spicy coconut milk sauce

1 fresh banana bud, or 13 oz (400 g)
  canned heart of palm
1/2 medium red onion, thinly sliced
6 cherry tomatoes, halved, or 1 small
  tomato, cut in small wedges
1 stem lemongrass, thinly sliced
1 fresh lime, cut in wedges
1 small cucumber, julienned
1 starfruit, thinly sliced
Few sprigs of basil (optional)

Spicy coconut milk sauce
1/2 medium red onion, chopped
1 large red chili, chopped
2 stems lemongrass, chopped
1 tablespoon vegetable oil
1/2 teaspoon dried shrimp paste,
  toasted
1 tablespoon fish curry powder
1/2 cup (125 ml) coconut milk
1 tablespoon coconut cream
5 oz (150 g) medium shrimps, peeled
  and deveined
1 teaspoon lime juice
1 teaspoon sugar
1/2 teaspoon salt

This exotic-sounding dish is a modern interpretation of a Nonya classic, developed by the Straits Chinese whose ancestors have lived for generations in Singapore and Malaysia. In this recipe, a spicy coconut milk sauce is poured over a salad of raw fruit and vegetables, cooked shrimps, and tender strips of banana bud, all served in banana petals.

1 Remove 4 reddish outside petals of the banana bud and set aside for serving. Peel off and discard the remaining outer leaves until you get to the paler colored tender inner portion. Put the banana bud in a large bowl of salted water with a weight on top and soak 4 hours, or overnight. Drain.
2 Bring a large saucepan of lightly salted water to a boil and add the banana bud. Simmer until tender when tested with a skewer, about 20 minutes. Drain, cool, then cut in half lengthways. Cut across in thin slices, pulling away any strands of sap and pinching the tips of the long enclosed flowers to remove and discard the hard filament inside.
3 Process the onion, chili, and lemongrass to a smooth paste. Heat the oil in a saucepan and add the paste. Stir-fry over moderate heat until fragrant, 3 minutes. Add the dried shrimp paste and curry powder and stir-fry for about 30 seconds. Slowly pour in the thin coconut milk and bring to a boil, stirring. Reduce heat and simmer until the liquid has reduced slightly, 3–4 minutes. Add the coconut cream, shrimps, lime juice, sugar, and salt and cook uncovered, stirring frequently, until the shrimps are just cooked, about 3 minutes.
4 Remove shrimps from the sauce. Divide the shrimps, shredded softened banana buds, onion, tomatoes, lemongrass, lime, cucumber, and starfruit, between 4 large banana petals (or serving dishes). Pour on the sauce and garnish with basil, if desired.

Ketchumbar salad

1 small Japanese cucumber, julienned
1 small carrot, julienned
1/2 small beetroot, julienned
1 medium tomato, seeded and
  julienned
1/2 capsicum, julienned
1 small onion, halved lengthways, thinly
  sliced across
1/4 cup (10 g) chopped fresh cilantro
  (coriander) leaves
1 tablespoon lime or lemon juice
4 teaspoons *chat masala*
1 teaspoon salt

Known in India and Maldives as *ketchumbar*, this salad is normally served as a side dish with rice, meat, and cooked vegetables or lentils, but can also be enjoyed as an appetizer (for a photograph of *ketchumbar*, see page 10). This salad makes an excellent accompaniment to shrimp *biryani* (see page 107).

1 Put all the vegetables, onion, and cilantro leaves in a bowl and sprinkle with the lime juice. Toss, then sprinkle over the *chat masala* and salt and toss again. Chill before serving.

Note: There should be about 3 1/2 oz (100 g) of each vegetable used in the salad. *Chat masala* is a distinctively flavoured, slightly sour Indian spice blend which should be available at Indian or specialty spice shops.

Vietnamese rice-paper rolls with tuna and fresh herbs

1/2 cup (25 g) fresh cilantro (coriander) leaves, finely chopped
1/2 cup (25 g) fresh Chinese celery leaves, finely chopped
1/2 cup (25 g) mint, finely chopped
1/2 cup (25 g) sweet or Thai basil, finely chopped
3 1/2 oz (100 g) sashimi-quality tuna
4 tablespoons XO sauce, oil drained off (see Note)
1 teaspoon pepper
2 teaspoons sugar
1/2 teaspoon sesame oil
16 small rice papers, about 6 in (16 cm) in diameter, or 10–12 large rice papers

Dipping sauce
1/4 cup (60 ml) fish sauce
1/4 cup (60 ml) lime or lemon juice
2 tablespoons very finely chopped garlic
6 large red chilies, seeded and very finely chopped
2 1/2 tablespoons white vinegar
3/4 cup (185 ml) water

This unusual version of the popular Vietnamese rice-paper rolls contains a mixture of the freshest possible sashimi-quality tuna with lashings of fragrant herbs and a luxurious sauce with a touch of aged brandy. The dipping sauce has plenty of garlic, seeded chili (so it is quite mild), fish sauce, and lime, making this a wonderfully piquant appetizer. This recipe can also be used to make equally delicious chicken and shrimp rice paper rolls (see Note).

1 Prepare the dipping sauce by combining all ingredients in a small bowl, stirring to mix well. To save time, you may use bottled Thai sweet chili sauce which is also an ideal partner for these rice-paper rolls.
2 Put the tuna, herbs, sauce, salt, pepper, and sesame oil in a bowl and stir to mix well. Dip a rice paper in a bowl of warm water for a few seconds until it starts to soften. Remove and place on a kitchen towel. Smooth the rice paper with your fingers. Repeat with a second rice paper.
3 Arrange about 2 tablespoons of the tuna mixture across the center of a rice paper, to within 3/4 in (2 cm) of each side. Roll up the rice paper, tucking in the edges to make a cigar shape and completely enclose the filling. Repeat with the remaining rice papers. Divide the rolls between 4 plates and put the sauce into 4 separate sauce bowls. Serve immediately.

Note: XO sauce is a blend of dried prawns, shallots, garlic, chili, and aged brandy; substitute with any Asian *sambal* or sauce that contains dried shrimps, garlic, and chili, adjusting the amount of sauce to taste depending upon the amount of chili contained. An alternative to tuna rolls is chicken and shrimp rolls. Blanch 10 oz (300 g) minced chicken breast and finely chop 10 oz (300 g) peeled and cooked shrimps, and substitute for the tuna in the recipe.

Fragrant crab cakes with sweet chili mayonnaise

4 oz (125 g) white-fleshed fish (such as
  snapper, bream or grouper), cubed
2 cups (250 g) cooked crabmeat,
  picked over for any cartilage
1 teaspoon very finely chopped garlic
1 teaspoon very finely chopped fresh
  ginger
1 stem lemongrass, very finely chopped
1/4 cup (10 g) firmly packed finely
  sliced Thai basil
1/4 cup (10 g) firmly packed finely
  chopped fresh cilantro (coriander)
  leaves
1 scallion (spring onion), finely chopped
4 teaspoons light soy sauce
4 teaspoons sesame oil
2 teaspoons fish sauce
1–3 teaspoons hot chili sauce
1/4 cup (75 g) finely diced red bell
  pepper (capsicum)
1/4 cup (75 g) finely diced yellow or
  green bell pepper (capsicum)
1 egg, lightly beaten
1/2 cup (60 g) all-purpose (plain) flour
1 cup (100 g) breadcrumbs
1/4 cup (60 ml) vegetable oil
Fresh watercress to garnish
1 red bell pepper (capsicum), roasted,
  cut in strips, to garnish

Sweet chili mayonnaise
3 tablespoons vegetable oil
2 shallots, chopped
1 clove garlic, chopped
2 tablespoons small dried shrimp,
  soaked in hot water 10 minutes,
  drained
1–2 teaspoons dried chili flakes
1 teaspoon finely chopped palm sugar
  or soft brown sugar
2 teaspoons fish sauce
1 tablespoon tamarind pulp, soaked in
  1/4 cup (60 ml) warm water, squeezed
  and strained to obtain juice
1/4 cup (60 ml) mayonnaise
1 teaspoon lime juice
Salt and pepper to taste

If you can obtain fresh crabmeat for these excellent savories, the result will be sublime. But even with other types of crabmeat, these herb-scented cakes accented with soy, sesame, fish sauce, and chili sauce will have people coming back for more. The unusual dip which accompanies the crab cakes is an East-West blend of mayonnaise, dried shrimps, fish sauce, and lime. This recipe is so good you may want to make double quantities and serve the crab cakes as a main course.

1 To prepare the sweet chili mayonnaise, heat oil in a small pan and stir-fry the shallots, garlic, and dried shrimp over low-moderate heat until cooked, about 4 minutes. Add chili, palm sugar, and tamarind juice and stir until the sugar has dissolved. Cool, then process to a smooth paste. Combine with mayonnaise and lime juice, then add salt and pepper to taste.
2 To make the crab cakes, process fish until finely minced. Add crab, the herbs, soy sauce, sesame oil, fish sauce, and chili sauce and pulse several times to mix well. Transfer mixture to a bowl and stir in the diced bell pepper. (If the mixture seems too moist, stir in 2–3 tablespoons breadcrumbs.) Shape mixture to make 12 small patties. Dip each in flour, then into the beaten egg, and coat well with the breadcrumbs. Refrigerate 30 minutes.
3 Heat 2 tablespoons of the oil and add half the crab cakes. Fry over moderate heat, about 2–3 minutes on each side, until golden brown and cooked. Drain on paper towel and repeat with remaining crab cakes. Serve hot with the mayonnaise and garnish with watercress and roasted bell pepper strips, if desired.

Candlelit walkways—Four Seasons Resort Bali at Jimbaran Bay

Spicy grilled snapper fillets with shallot and lemongrass sambal

4 boneless snapper fillets, each about
  5 oz (150 g)
Salt and pepper to taste
4 teaspoons lime or lemon juice
4 pieces banana leaf, each about 9 in
  (22 cm) square, softened in a gas
  flame or boiling water
1 small green tomato, sliced
2 kaffir lime leaves, halved
2 tablespoons lemon basil leaves
1 *salam* leaf, cut in 4 (optional)

Spice paste
2 tablespoons vegetable oil
8–10 shallots, finely chopped
4–5 cloves garlic, finely chopped
2 red or green bird's-eye chilies,
  chopped
1 tablespoon finely chopped galangal
1 tablespoon finely chopped fresh
  ginger
1 teaspoon finely chopped turmeric, or
  1/2 teaspoon turmeric powder
3 stems lemongrass, finely chopped
1 teaspoon dried shrimp paste
2 teaspoons finely chopped palm sugar
1 tablespoon tamarind pulp, soaked in
  1/4 cup (60 ml) warm water, squeezed
  and strained to obtain juice
1/2 teaspoon salt
Freshly ground black pepper to taste

Shallot and lemongrass *sambal*
1/2 teaspoon dried shrimp paste, toasted
2 teaspoons peanut or vegetable oil
1 tablespoon lime or lemon juice
1/2 teaspoon salt
Freshly ground black pepper to taste
8–10 shallots, very thinly sliced
10 stems lemongrass, very thinly sliced
10 kaffir lime leaves, very finely
  shredded
1 large red chili, seeds discarded, very
  finely chopped
1–3 red or green bird's-eye chilies, sliced

Pepes ikan—fish slathered with a fragrant spice paste and wrapped in banana leaf for steaming or grilling—is one of the most delicious dishes in the Balinese culinary repertoire. The spice paste can be prepared in advance and refrigerated, but for maximum fragrance, the accompanying *sambal* of chilies, shallots, lemongrass, and kaffir lime should be made only while the fish is grilling.

1 Prepare the spice paste first. Heat the oil in a small pan and add shallots, garlic, chilies, galangal, ginger, turmeric powder, lemongrass, and shrimp paste. Stir-fry over low-medium heat until fragrant, 4–5 minutes. Add the remaining ingredients and cook, stirring frequently until soft, 6–8 minutes. Cool, then grind or process to a smooth paste.
2 Place the fish fillets on a plate and season on both sides with salt, pepper, and lime juice. Spread the spice paste evenly over both sides of each fillet. Place a piece of banana leaf on a board or table, and put a fish fillet diagonally across the leaf. Top with some of the tomato, half a lime leaf, some of the basil leaves, and a quarter of the *salam* leaf. Fold over the end closest to you, tuck in the sides and then turn over to enclose the filling. Repeat with remaining fish fillets.
3 Place banana leaf packages over hot charcoal and grill on both sides until the fish is done, about 8 minutes altogether, depending on the thickness of the fish.
4 While the fish is grilling, prepare the shallot and lemongrass *sambal* by mixing the toasted shrimp paste with the lime juice, oil, salt, and pepper until dissolved. Then add the remaining ingredients and mix well.
5 Serve the fish in its banana leaf package (diners must be unwrap the leaf, it cannot be eaten), accompanied by the *sambal* and steamed white rice.

Bali's celebrated gamelan orchestra—Jimbaran Bay

Bali-style sushi: spicy chicken and mango sushi, red rice and tempe sushi, shrimp and sambal sushi, nori roll with vegetables

Sushi rice
1 1/2 cups (400 g) short-grain Calrose or sushi rice
2 cups (500 ml) water
1 piece *kombu* seaweed, 2 1/2-in (6-cm) square
3 tablespoons rice vinegar
3 tablespoons sugar
1 tablespoon *mirin*
1 1/2 teaspoons salt

Spicy chicken and mango sushi
2 tablespoons vegetable oil
2 shallots, finely chopped
4 cloves garlic, finely chopped
2–3 large red chilies, sliced
1 bird's-eye chili, sliced
1/2 teaspoon dried shrimp paste, toasted
1/2 teaspoon salt
Liberal sprinkling white pepper
2 sheets sushi *nori*, 7 1/4 x 8 1/4 in (18 1/2 x 21 cm)
1 3/4 cups (350 g) cooked sushi rice
1 3/4 oz (50 g) cooked chicken breast, finely shredded
1 3/4 oz (50 g) finely julienned firm ripe mango
3/4 oz (25 g) finely julienned red bell pepper (capsicum)

Red rice and *tempe* sushi
2 teaspoons vegetable oil
1 shallot, very finely chopped
1 clove garlic, very finely choped
1 large red chili, seeded and finely shredded
1 bird's-eye chili, finely chopped
1 3/4 oz (50 g) fermented soybean cake (*tempe*), finely julienned and deep-fried until crisp
2 tablespoons sweet soy sauce (*kecap manis*)
2 teaspoons oyster sauce
1 teaspoon finely chopped palm sugar or soft brown sugar
1/2 teaspoon salt
1 tablespoon tamarind pulp, soaked in 2 tablespoons warm water, squeezed and strained to obtain juice
2 sheets sushi *nori*, 7 1/4 x 8 1/4 in (18 1/2 x 21 cm)
1 3/4 oz (50 g) finely julienned seeded cucumber
1/2 cup (100 g) red or "hill" rice, boiled until cooked
3/4 cup (150 g) cooked sushi rice

These recipes are a creative Balinese interpretation of Japanese sushi. You could always try just one or two of these sushi if you don't have time to prepare them all. For remaining sushi recipes, see page 184.

Sushi rice
1 Put the rice, water, and *kombu* in a pan, cover and bring to a boil. Discard *kombu* and cover saucepan, leaving the lid slightly open. Cook over moderate heat until the water is completely absorbed, about 5 minutes. Cook over minimum heat, 10 minutes. Wipe inside the saucepan lid, cover and remove from heat. Let stand for 10 minutes.
2 Stir vinegar, sugar, *mirin*, and salt in a small bowl until sugar is dissolved. Transfer cooked rice into a wide bowl and toss gently with a wooden spoon, gradually pouring over the dressing. Toss frequently until the rice has cooled slightly, 5 minutes. Set aside until completely cold, about 20 minutes. This recipe makes 5 cups (800 g) cooked sushi rice.

Spicy chicken and mango sushi
1 Heat oil and stir-fry shallots, garlic, both lots of chilies, and shrimp paste over low-medium heat until soft and cooked, 7–8 minutes. Cool, then pound or process to a paste and set aside.
2 Lay a piece of plastic wrap on top of a split bamboo sushi mat. Wet your hands. Spread half the rice mixture in a rectangle about 5 in (12 cm) wide across the plastic, pressing it firmly with the spoon and your hands to compact the rice slightly; make sure the rice is spread to each side of the sushi mat. Spread half the spice paste in a thin line down the center of the rice, then top this with half the chicken, mango, and capsicum. Roll up firmly using the mat, to enclose the filling completely with the rice. Remove the roll from the mat, then carefully remove plastic and place the roll across 1 sheet of *nori*. Roll up firmly. Repeat with the remaining *nori*, rice, spice paste and filling. Cut each roll across with a sharp knife into 5–6 pieces. Serve with pickled ginger, *wasabi*, and soy sauce.

Red rice and *tempe* sushi
1 Heat oil in a wok and add shallot, garlic, and both lots of chilies. Stir-fry over low-medium heat, 3 minutes. Add *tempe*, soy sauce, oyster sauce, palm sugar, salt, and tamarind juice and stir-fry until the liquid dries up, about 2 minutes. Remove mixture with a slotted spoon, leaving any oil in the wok, and allow mixture to cool.
2 Combine red rice and sushi rice, stirring to mix well. Set aside.
3 Place the *nori* sheets on a board and arrange half the *tempe* mixture and cucumber across from side to side down the center of each sheet. Roll up very firmly and set aside.
4 Wet your hands. Use a spoon to spread half the rice mixture in a rectangle about 5 in (12 cm) wide across a sushi mat, pressing it firmly with the spoon and your hands to make it adhere and making sure the rice is spread to each side of the sushi mat. Lay one *nori*-wrapped roll in the center. Roll up, squeezing firmly, so that the *nori* roll is completely enclosed by the rice. Set roll aside and repeat with remaining rice and *nori*-wrapped roll. Cut each roll across with a sharp knife into 5 pieces. Serve with pickled ginger, *wasabi*, and soy sauce.

Pita bread pockets

4 pita bread
2 lettuce leaves, washed, dried and
  finely shredded
2 long white Chinese (napa) cabbage
  leaves, washed, dried and finely
  shredded
1/2 medium tomato, julienned
1/2 small onion, julienned
1 teaspoon lime juice
1/2 teaspoon salt
4 sprigs fresh cilantro (coriander) leaves
  to garnish
4 sprigs mint to garnish
Red chili, sliced, to garnish

Filling
6 1/2 oz (200 g) grilled garlic and
  coriander chicken breast (below), grilled
  beef with *rendang* marinade (page
  126), or grilled lemongrass marinated
  lamb chops (page 179), shredded

Fresh salad vegetables, accentuated by an accompanying flavored *raita* (page 172), are partnered with your choice of beef, chicken, or lamb. When preparing meat recipes for another meal, make sure you cook extra so you'll have plenty extra for these pita breads.

1 Prepare a flavored *raita* (see page 172).
2 Cut each pita bread across in half, so you have 8 pockets. Combine lettuce, cabbage, tomato, onion, lime juice, and salt in a bowl, tossing to coat well. Divide this salad between the bread pockets, then add some of the beef, chicken, or lamb. Garnish with cilantro, mint, and red chili, and serve with a flavored *raita*, if desired.

Grilled garlic and coriander chicken breast

4 skinless chicken breasts, each about
  5–6 oz (150–180 g)
4 sprigs fresh cilantro (coriander) leaves
6–8 baby leeks, grilled

Marinade
4 teaspoons coriander seeds, lightly
  toasted
4 teaspoons cumin seeds, lightly toasted
5–6 cloves garlic, very finely chopped
2 tablespoons finely chopped fresh
  cilantro (coriander) leaves
4 teaspoons paprika
2 teaspoons chili powder
1 teaspoon salt
1/4 teaspoon freshly ground black
  pepper
2 tablespoons vegetable oil

1 For the marinade, process the coriander and cumin seeds to a fine powder in a spice grinder. Transfer to a bowl and stir in all other ingredients. Spread both sides of the chicken with the marinade, and set aside for 30 minutes or longer.
2 Brush a grill with oil and cook the chicken breasts over a medium fire, turning to cook both sides. Serve with a sprig of cilantro and baby leeks, or in pita bread.

Naan basket with mango and banana chutneys and raita

Naan
3/4 teaspoon superfine (caster) sugar
1/4 cup (50 ml) warm water
1 teaspoon instant yeast
2 cups (250 g) all-purpose (plain) flour
1/2 teaspoon salt
1/3 cup (85 ml) water
2 tablespoons plain yogurt
1 tablespoon melted butter

Spiced mango chutney
1 1/4 cups (200 g) peeled and diced
  unripe mango
2 1/2 cups (240 g) grated coconut
4 green chilies, sliced
1/2 teaspoon salt
1 1/2 tablespoons oil
1/2 teaspoon urad dhal
1/2 teaspoon mustard seeds
1 sprig curry leaves
1/4 teaspoon asafoetida (optional)

Banana chutney (see page 45)

Mixed vegetable raita
1/3 cup (50 g) very finely diced mixed
  vegetables, such as cucumber, onion,
  carrot, tomato, green and red bell
  pepper (capsicum)
1 tablespoon finely chopped fresh
  cilantro (coriander) leaves
1/2 teaspoon cumin powder
1/2 teaspoon salt
125 ml (1/2 cup) thick plain yogurt,
  chilled

Accompaniments
Crudité of sliced raw vegetables and
  fruit such as coconut, cucumber,
  carrot, bell pepper (capsicum)
Lemon wedges

An excellent dish to serve at parties, flavored *naan* is accompanied by a simple crudité of raw vegetables and fruit, and a selection of chutneys and *raita*.

1 To prepare the *naan*. Put sugar and warm water in a bowl and sprinkle over the yeast. Leave in a warm place until it is dissolved and frothy, about 10 minutes.
2 Sift flour and salt in a bowl, then make a well in the center. Pour in the yeast mixture, water, yogurt, and butter, stirring to make a soft dough. Add a little more flour if the dough seems sticky. Turn out and knead on a lightly floured surface for 10–15 minutes, until the dough is smooth and elastic. Lightly oil the mixing bowl, add dough and cover loosely with plastic and cover the bowl with a kitchen towel. Leave in a warm place until dough doubles in size, about 1 hour.
3 When the *naan* dough has risen, divide into 4 pieces. Shape each into a ball, cover and leave to rise on a lightly floured surface, about 30 minutes. Flatten the balls with the hands, then roll into circles about 7 in (18 cm) in diameter. Place on a floured surface, cover with a kitchen towel and leave to rise until spongy and light to the touch, about 20 minutes. (See Note for flavored *naan*.)
4 Heat a heavy skillet until hot. Add a piece of dough and cover the pan and cook for 2 minutes. Turn the dough and cook the other side, again with the pan covered. Wrap in a kitchen towel while cooking the remaining *naan*.
5 To make the mango chutney, coarsley grind the diced mango, coconut, chilies, and salt, then set aside. In a small saucepan, over a low flame, heat the oil and sauté the *urad dhal* until golden brown. Add the mustard seeds and curry leaves and sauté until the mustard seeds pop. Add the asafoetida, if using, mix and remove from heat. Transfer the fried spices to the ground chutney and mix well.
6 To prepare the mixed vegetable *raita*, combine the vegetables, cilantro, cumin, salt, and yogurt in a bowl, stirring to mix well. Serve immediately, or cover and refrigerate up to 1 hour. (If liked, the *raita* could be made using cucumber only.)
7 To serve, place the *naan* and the various accompaniments in separate bowls and let guests choose their own dips.

Note: To make garlic *naan*, sprinkle minced garlic and chopped fresh cilantro (coriander) leaves on the dough before cooking. For Kashmiri *naan*, sprinkle 2 tablespoons saffron milk (made by soaking 1/4 teaspoon saffron threads in 2 tablespoons hot milk), 1 tablespoon sesame seeds, and 2 tablespoons raisins on the dough before cooking. Experiment using your own favorite blend of spices and dried fruits.

Assorted satay with peanut sauce and pineapple sambal

8 oz (250 g) chicken breast or fillet, cut
  in 1 1/4-in (3-cm) cubes
13 oz (400 g) raw medium shrimps,
  peeled, tail section left intact

Marinade
3 tablespoons vegetable oil
6 shallots, finely chopped
5–6 cloves garlic, finely chopped
1 tablespoon finely chopped fresh ginger
2 teaspoons finely chopped turmeric
3 stems lemongrass, very thinly sliced
2 teaspoons honey
1 teaspoon salt

Peanut sauce
2 tablespoons vegetable oil
3 shallots, finely chopped
2 cloves garlic, finely chopped
2 large red chilies, finely chopped
1/2 teaspoon dried shrimp paste, toasted
2 kaffir lime leaves
1 1/2 teaspoons finely chopped aromatic
  ginger (*kencur/cekur*) or fresh ginger
2 tablespoons finely chopped palm
  sugar or soft brown sugar
1 tablespoon tamarind pulp, soaked in
  1/4 cup (60 ml) warm water, squeezed
  and strained to obtain juice
1 tablespoon sugar
1 teaspoon salt
Freshly ground black pepper to taste
1 cup (250 ml) water
3/4 cup (125 g) peanuts, dry-roasted,
  skinned and finely ground

Pineapple *sambal*
2 tablespoons vegetable oil
5 cloves garlic, sliced
4 shallots, sliced
1 large red chili, sliced
1 red or green bird's-eye chili, sliced
6 1/2 oz (200 g) finely diced fresh
  pineapple
1 teaspoon dried shrimp paste, toasted
  and crushed
1/2 teaspoon salt
1/2 teaspoon sugar

Satay in Southeast Asia ranges from simple skewers of grilled meat served with a dip of sweet soy sauce and sliced chilies to sophisticated versions like this. Chicken breast cubes and shrimps are marinated in an aromatic paste before being grilled, and are served with a thick, slightly sweet peanut sauce and an intriguing sweet-sour-spicy pineapple *sambal*. This makes a most impressive appetizer.

1 To prepare the marinade, heat oil in a small pan and add the shallots, garlic, ginger, turmeric, and lemongrass. Stir-fry over low heat until fragrant and cooked, about 8 minutes. Cool, then blend to a smooth paste. Transfer to a bowl and stir in honey and salt. Set aside to cool, then stir in the chicken pieces and shrimps and marinate in the refrigerator for 3–4 hours.
2 To make the peanut sauce, heat the oil in a saucepan and stir-fry the shallots, garlic, chilies, shrimp paste, lime leaves, and aromatic ginger over low–moderate heat until fragrant, about 4 minutes. Add the palm sugar, tamarind juice, sugar, salt, pepper, and water, stirring well. Add the ground peanuts, bring to a boil and simmer, stirring from time to time, until the sauce has thickened, about 15 minutes. Discard the lime leaves and transfer sauce to a serving bowl.
3 Prepare the pineapple *sambal*. Heat the oil in a saucepan and add garlic, shallots, and chilies, 4–5 minutes. Add the pineapple and stir-fry 5 minutes, then stir in shrimp paste, salt, and sugar, mixing well. Remove from heat, cool, then process until smooth. Transfer to a serving dish.
4 Thread the marinated chicken pieces and shrimps on bamboo skewers. Cook over very hot charcoal, turning to cook and brown all over, 10–12 minutes.

Note: If you prefer to cook only one kind of satay, you may double the amount of the chicken or shrimps. Grill some skewered chilies, with the seeds removed, if you fancy a really hot appetizer!

Pizza topped with stir-fried lamb, arugula, and mozzarella

1 uncooked pizza base
1/2 cup (125 ml) canned tomato purée
3/4 cup (75 g) grated mozzarella cheese
1 large red chili, sliced
1/2 cup loosely packed shredded
 arugula/rucola leaves, or spinach
1 tablespoon crisp-fried garlic slices

Stir-fried lamb
2 teaspoons cornstarch
1/4 cup (60 ml) water
2 teaspoons *hoisin* sauce
2 teaspoons oyster sauce
1 teaspoon light soy sauce
1 teaspoon chili sauce
1 tablespoon vegetable oil
2 cloves garlic, finely chopped
3 1/2 oz (100 g) lamb fillet, very thinly
 sliced
1 large red chili, sliced
1 large green chili, sliced
1 tablespoon finely chopped fresh
 cilantro (coriander) leaves

Pizza base
1 teaspoon instant dry yeast
Pinch of sugar or a little honey
2/3 cup (160 ml) tepid water, more as
 needed
2 cups (250 g) all-purpose (plain) flour
Pinch of salt
1 tablespoon olive oil

This pizza has a distinctive Chinese flavor, thanks to the traditional sauces and seasonings used to cook the topping of stir-fry sliced lamb. The lamb is partnered with the more customary Italian tomato sauce and mozzarella cheese, the result being a delicious combination of East and West.

1 To prepare the stir-fried lamb, combine cornstarch and water in a small bowl and set aside. Mix *hoisin*, oyster, soy, and chili sauces together and set aside. Heat oil in a wok and stir-fry garlic until fragrant, about 10 seconds. Add lamb and stir-fry over high heat, 30 seconds. Add the sauce mixture and chilies and stir-fry a further 30 seconds. Stir in the cornstarch mixture and cook until it thickens and clears, about 30 seconds. Stir in cilantro, then transfer to plate.
2 If making a homemade pizza base, combine the yeast, sugar, and water in bowl and set aside until it starts to bubble. Sift the flour and salt into a large mixing bowl and make a well in the center. Pour the frothy yeast mixture and olive oil into the well and mix to form a smooth dough. Knead the dough on a lightly dusted work surface for about 5 minutes. Transfer the dough to a clean, oiled bowl and leave to stand in a warm place until it has doubled in size, about 30 minutes or more depending on the conditions. Punch the dough to knock the air out of it, then roll out into a thin circle about 10 in (25 cm) in diameter.
3 Put the pizza base on an oven tray or pizza plate and spread with the tomato purée. Sprinkle with the cheese, spread the stir-fried lamb evenly on top, then scatter with the sliced red chili. Bake in a very hot oven until crisp and cooked, about 12–15 minutes. Before serving, scatter with the arugula and garlic and cut into slices.

Grilled lemongrass-marinated lamb chops

4 double lamb loin chops, or 8 single
   lamb loin chops, trimmed of excess
   fat
Freshly ground black pepper to taste
8 pods fresh or frozen green soy beans,
   boiled until tender, shells discarded

Marinade
2 teaspoons cumin seeds, lightly toasted
3 in (8 cm) fresh ginger, chopped
1 1/2 in (4 cm) fresh turmeric, chopped
4 shallots, chopped
4 cloves garlic, chopped
4 stems lemongrass, sliced
2 tablespoons sugar
1 teaspoon salt
2 tablespoons vegetable oil

The heavenly perfume of lemongrass, processed to a paste with
other aromatics and cumin, permeates these lamb chops. As they
can be prepared well in advance, they're ideal to serve at a barbecue
or picnic, and can be accompanied by either baby new potatoes
or rice.

1 To prepare the marinade, grind the cumin seeds to a fine powder in a spice
grinder. Add all other ingredients except oil and process to a smooth paste,
adding a little of the oil if needed to keep the mixture turning.
2 Heat the oil in a small pan and stir-fry the paste over low heat until fragrant
and cooked, 8–10 minutes. Transfer to a bowl and leave to cool.
3 Sprinkle both sides of the lamb chops with a little freshly ground pepper,
then rub generously with the marinade. Set aside to marinate for 30 minutes
or longer. Grill the chops until done to taste and serve garnished with the
cooked green soy beans. Slice the meat from any leftover chops to be eaten
in pita bread, see page 171.

Note: If green soy bean pods are not available, garnish the lamb with
6 1/2 oz (200 g) cooked lima beans, boiled spinach or sprigs of fresh
watercress.

Barbecue in the padi field—Four Seasons Resort Bali at Sayan

Tropical salad with spicy palm sugar sauce

5 oz (150 g) water apple, cut in
wedges, or 1 starfruit, sliced
5 oz (150 g) firm ripe papaya, peeled
and cut in large dice
5 oz (150 g) pineapple, peeled and cut
into bite-sized wedges
5 oz (150 g) jicama (yam bean), or
1 *salak* (snake fruit), peeled and cut
in large dice
1 unripe green mango, peeled, stoned
and flesh, thinly sliced

Spicy palm sugar sauce
1/4 cup (60 g) tamarind pulp
Scant 1/2 cup (100 g) chopped palm
sugar or soft brown sugar
3/4 cup (185 ml) water
1/2 teaspoon salt
4 bird's-eye chilies, chopped
1 teaspoon dried shrimp paste, toasted

Little distinction is made between fruits and vegetables in the tropics, with avocados eaten with sugar or condensed milk, and pineapple eaten with salt or hot spicy dips. In Indonesia, Malaysia, and Singapore, a mixture of refreshing fruits and crunchy vegetables is tossed with a tamarind and palm sugar syrup accented with chili and shrimp paste to make a delightfully different salad, known locally as *rujak*.

1 To make the sauce, combine tamarind, sugar, water, and salt in a small saucepan. Bring to a boil, stirring until sugar dissolves, then lower heat and simmer uncovered until the mixture thickens and turns syrupy, 12–15 minutes. Strain into a bowl, pressing on the pulp to obtain as much juice as possible. Pound or process salt, chilies, and shrimp paste to a paste. Stir in to the syrup and allow to cool before using.
2 Just before the salad is required, combine water apple, papaya, pineapple, jicama, and mango in a bowl. Pour over the syrup and toss to mix well.

Note: It is important to toast the dried shrimp paste thoroughly. An easy way to do this is to press the paste into a thin wafer on a piece of foil. Wrap and put it in the bottom of a wok, pressing down so the foil contacts the base of the wok. Cook over moderate heat, turning the foil, until the shrimp paste is paler in color, dry, and crumbly; this will take 6–8 minutes.

Salak (snake fruit)

Banana, chocolate, and mint samosa

2 cups (250 g) all-purpose (plain) flour,
  plus extra for kneading
2 tablespoons vegetable oil
1/2 cup (125 ml) water
8 small strips pandan (screwpine) leaf
Vegetable oil for deep-frying
4 tablespoons tropical fruit purée
  (mango, passionfruit, or papaya)

Filling
3/4 cup (125 g) white or dark chocolate,
  grated
4 bananas, each about 3 1/2 oz (100 g)
1 tablespoon finely chopped mint

This recipe could be seen as a variation on the Western after-dinner mint, the perennial mint-flavored chocolate. In this case, fresh mint and grated chocolate are mashed with banana, wrapped in a light pastry and deep-fried to make a most unusual dessert. You can prepare the *samosa* in advance and refrigerate them, doing the final brief deep-frying just before serving.

1 Sift the flour into a bowl. Make a well in the center and pour in the oil and water. Stir to incorporate the liquid, then knead the dough on a floured board for about 10 minutes until soft but not sticky, adding a little extra flour if needed. Divide dough into 8 balls, then flatten each with the hand. Roll out each disc of dough to a circle about 5 1/2 in (14 cm) in diameter.
2 Prepare the filling by mashing chocolate, bananas, and mint together. (If working in a hot climate, put the filling in the freezer for 5 minutes to chill the chocolate.) Put about 1 tablespoon of the filling in the center of each circle and lift the edge of the dough circle to enclose the filling. Dab a little water on the inside of the neck area to help it stick and tie a small strip of pandan leaf around the outside of the neck.
3 Heat oil in a wok until moderately hot. Deep-fry the *samosa*, a few at a time, until golden brown, 2–3 minutes. Drain on paper towel and serve hot or warm, with 1 tablespoon of fruit purée on each serving plate.

A typical day at Four Seasons Resort Maldives

additional recipes

Fresh coconut chutney for masala dosai

2 1/2 cups (200 g) freshly grated or
   moistened desiccated coconut
1/2 cup (20 g) fresh mint leaves
1 large green chili, chopped
1 teaspoon salt
1/3 cup (85 ml) water
2 tablespoons oil
1 teaspoon brown mustard seeds
8 curry leaves, sliced
1/2 small onion, very finely chopped

Fresh coconut chutney is an ideal accompaniment for *masala dosai*, see recipe on page 30.

Process the coconut, mint, chili, salt, and water to a smooth paste and set aside. Heat the oil in a small saucepan and stir-fry the mustard seed, onion, and curry leaves over low-moderate heat until onion is soft, 3–4 minutes. Pour the fried onions and spices over the fresh chutney and stir to mix.

Shrimp and sambal sushi & Balinese vegetable nori roll

Shrimp and *sambal* sushi
4 medium shrimps
1 tablespoon vegetable oil
1 shallot, thinly sliced
2 teaspoons finely chopped lemon grass
1 small bird's-eye chili, finely chopped
1/4 teaspoon dried shrimp paste,
   toasted and mashed
1/4 teaspoon salt
Liberal sprinkling white pepper
3/4 cup (150 g) cooked sushi rice
1 tablespoon very finely shredded
   green papaya or 8 bean sprouts
1/2 large red chili, very finely shredded
1 small kaffir lime leaf, finely shredded
5 cm (2 in) scallion (spring onion)
   greens, very finely shredded

Balinese vegetable *nori* roll
1 tablespoon vegetable oil
3 cloves garlic, finely chopped
2 teaspoons finely chopped aromatic
   ginger (*kencur*)
2 teaspoons finely chopped turmeric
1/2 teaspoon ground black pepper
2 tablespoons coconut milk
1/4 teaspoon salt
1 tablespoon finely julienned carrot
1 tablespoon julienned baby corn
1 tablespoon finely julienned red chili
1 long bean, or 2 green beans, cut in
   2-in (5-cm) lengths, blanched
2 large spinach leaves, finely julienned
1 leaf long whitee Chines (napa)
   cabbage, finely shredded
1 tablespoon desiccated coconut,
   toasted until golden brown
2 teaspoons crisp-fried shallots
1/4 teaspoon lime juice
1 sheet sushi nori, 7 x 8 in (18 x 21 cm)
Scant 1 cup (180 g) cooked sushi rice

Our Balinese sushi is a fun twist on this favorite of Japanese foods. For more Bali-style sushi recipes and for a sushi rice recipe, see page 168.

Shrimp and *sambal* sushi
1 Push a toothpick or part of a bamboo skewer through the shrimp, from the back of the head to the tail, to hold it straight during cooking. Bring 1 cup (250 ml) lightly salted water to a boil, add the shrimps and simmer 3 minutes. Drain, cool, and peel the cooked shrimps and remove the dark vein. Cut down the underside of each with a sharp knife, then press gently with the palm of the hand to spread open or "butterfly" each shrimp. Set aside.
2 Process the oil, shallot, lemon grass, bird's-eye chili, shrimp paste, salt, and pepper to a paste.
3 Divide the sushi rice into 4 portions, and squeeze each firmly with wet hands to make a compact oblong about 2 in (5 cm) long. Press with the side of the finger in the center of each piece of rice to make a slight depression. Fill with a little of the spice paste, papaya shreds (or 2 bean sprouts), a few shreds of chili, and a few shreds of scallion greens. Top each portion with a shrimp and serve immediately.

Balinese vegetable *nori* roll
1 Heat oil in a small saucepan, then add garlic, aromatic ginger, turmeric, and pepper. Stir-fry over low-moderate heat until cooked, 6–8 minutes. Cool, then process to a paste. Returning paste to the pan, stir in coconut milk and salt and heat, stirring. Transfer paste to a large bowl and set aside until cool.
2 Add carrot, corn, chili, beans, spinach, cabbage, coconut, shallots, and lime juice to the paste and toss to mix well.
3 Lay a piece of plastic wrap on top of a split bamboo sushi mat. Wet your hands. Spread the rice mixture in a rectangle about 5-in (12-cm) wide across the plastic, pressing it firmly with the spoon and your hands to compact the rice slightly; make sure the rice is spread to each side of the sushi mat. Arrange the vegetable mixture down the centre of the rice, then roll up firmly using the mat to enclose the filling completely with the rice.
4 Remove the roll from the mat, then carefully remove plastic and place the roll across 1 sheet of *nori*. Roll up firmly. Cut across with a sharp knife into 5–6 pieces before serving.

Balinese-style mixed vegetables, tempe, and sweet sambal

Balinese-style mixed vegetables
2 cups (500 ml) water
1 teaspoon salt
2 cups (120 g) fern tips, or young
  pea sprouts (*dao miao*), or water
  cress
2 cups (120 g) spinach leaves
1 cup young green beans, cut in
  2-cm (1-in) lengths
1 cup (100 g) bean sprouts, straggly
  tails discarded
1/2 cup (50 g) freshly grated or
  moistened desiccated coconut
1 large red chili, finely julienned
2–3 bird's-eye chilies, sliced and
  deep-fried until crisp
2 cloves garlic, thinly sliced and
  deep-fried until crisp
1 tablespoon crisp-fried shallots
1/4 teaspoon salt
1/4 teaspoon ground black pepper
1/4 teaspoon dried shrimp paste,
  toasted and crushed
1 tablespoon lime juice

Dressing
2 tablespoons vegetable oil
2–3 cloves garlic, finely chopped
1 tablespoon finely chopped aromatic
  ginger (*kencur*)
1 teaspoon finely chopped turmeric
4 bird's-eye chilies, chopped
1/4 teaspoon salt
1/4 teaspoon freshly ground black
  pepper

Crispy *tempe*
1 teaspoon coriander seeds, lightly
  toasted
4 cloves garlic, chopped
2 red or green bird's-eye chilies, sliced
1/2 teaspoon salt
2 tablespoons water
150 g (5 oz) unseasoned fermented
  soybean cake (*tempe*), diced
Vegetable oil for deep-frying

Sweet *sambal*
3 tablespoons vegetable oil
6 shallots, chopped
4–5 cloves garlic, chopped
6–8 large red chilies, seeds discarded,
  chopped
2 red or green bird's-eye chilies,
  chopped
1 medium ripe tomato, chopped
2 teaspoons chopped palm sugar, or
  soft brown sugar
1 teaspoon dried shrimp paste,
  toasted
1 teaspoon salt
1/4 cup (60 ml) tomato ketchup
1/4 cup (60 ml) water

Balinese-style mixed vegetables, crispy *tempe*, pickled cucumber, and sweet *sambal* are components of the composite dish *nasi campur*, the recipe for which can be found on page 116.

Balinese-style mixed vegetables
1 Bring water and salt to a boil in a saucepan. Add fern tips and blanch for only 1 minute. Remove with a slotted spatula, plunge in cold water, drain and set aside. Repeat for the spinach leaves, squeezing firmly to remove excess water after cooling and draining. Blanch the beans for 2 minutes, drain and set aside. Blanch the bean sprouts 10 seconds only, then chill and drain.
2 Put vegetables, coconut, both lots of chilli, fried garlic, fried shallots, salt, and pepper in a bowl, tossing by hand to mix well. Refrigerate. Mix shrimp paste with lime juice, stirring to dissolve, then set aside until just before serving.
3 Make dressing by heating the oil in a small pan. Add all ingredients except salt and pepper and stir-fry over low-medium heat until fragrant, 3–4 minutes. Cool, then process to a smooth paste together with the salt and pepper. Just before serving, add the dressing and lime juice with shrimp paste to the vegetable mix and toss again.

Crispy *tempe*
Process the coriander seeds in a grinder until finely ground. Add garlic, chilies, and salt process to a paste, adding a little of the water if needed. Transfer to a bowl, stir in the water, then mix in the diced *tempe*. Set aside to marinate for 1 hour, stirring a couple of times. Heat oil in a wok and deep-fry the tempe over high heat until crisp and golden brown, about 2 minutes.

Sweet *sambal*
Heat oil in a small saucepan and add shallots, garlic, and both lots of chili. Stir-fry over low-moderate heat until fragrant, 3–4 minutes, then add tomato, palm sugar, and shrimp paste. Cook, stirring frequently, 5 minutes. Cool then process to a smooth paste. Return to the pan, stir in salt, tomato sauce, and water. Cook over low heat, stirring frequently for 10 minutes. Transfer to a bowl and serve at room temperature.

Pickled cucumber
Bring sugar, vinegar, water, ginger, and salt to a boil in a saucepan. Simmer 2 minutes, then allow to cool. Remove ginger and transfer liquid to a bowl. Halve cucumbers lengthways, discard seeds and cut across in 1/2-in (1 cm) slices. Add cucumber, chilies, and shallots to cooled syrup, mixing well. Cover and refrigerate 2 hours before serving.

Pickled cucumber
1/3 cup (85 g) sugar
2 tablespoons white vinegar
1 cup (250 ml) water
2 in (5 cm) fresh ginger, smashed
1–1 1/2 teaspoons salt
2 small Japanese cucumbers, skin raked
  with a fork, or 6 1/2 oz (200 g) regular
  cucumber
5–8 green bird's-eye chilies, left whole,
  bruised
2 shallots, thinly sliced

glossary

Ajowan: Also known as carom, ajowan is a plant of the same family as caraway and parsely whose seeds are a popular flavoring in India and the Middle East. Sometimes sold under its Indian name, *ajwain*.

Aromatic ginger: With no standard English name, this plant is known as *kencur* in Indonesia, *cekur* in Malaysia, and *pro hom* in Thailand. The rhizome is used to flavor dishes while the leaves may be used either as a flavoring in cooked dishes or eaten raw as a herb in salads.

Asam gelugor: These dried sour slices, also known as *asam keping* in Malay and Indonesian, and *som khaek* in Thai, are used as a souring agent in some Southeast Asian dishes. Since the flavor imparted is only subtly different to that of tamarind, both are interchangeable in these recipes. See tamarind.

Banana bud: Popular throughout Southeast Asia as a vegetable, the banana bud is the tapering, purple-red inflorescence that hangs at the end of a clump of bananas. The outer leaves are removed, together with the blossoms, to reveal the pinkish-white heart. Using an oiled knife, cut the bud lengthways into four. The bud can then be chopped and blanched depending on the recipe.

Basil, Thai: This very fragrant form of basil is known as *horapa* in Thailand, and is often sold in the west as "Asian basil." It has pinkish purple flowers and a purplish tinge to the bright green leaves. **Sweet basil** may be used as a substitute for Thai basil.

Bean sprouts: The most common variety is sprouted mung beans although sprouted soya beans can also be found. Mung bean sprouts are crisp and crunchy and have a delicate, slightly sweet taste while soya bean sprouts are twice as large and possess a stronger bean flavor. Store in the refrigerator, covered with water, for up to 3 days for mung bean sprouts and 5 days for soya bean sprouts, changing the water daily.

Candlenut: A relative of the macadamia nut, the candlenut (*buah keras* in Malay, *kemiri* in Indonesian) is not eaten raw but is used, pounded, in cooked dishes such as curries to add texture and flavor.

Cardamom: Both the greenish pods and the black seeds inside may be used (the pods are not eaten if used whole). Readily available from Indian foodstores.

Cassava (tapioca): The tender young leaves, starchy tubers, and young roots may be eaten. Not to be confused with yam beans, sweet potatoes, or taro.

Chat masala: This unique, sour and pungent blend of spices, dried mango, and black salt is popular in Indian cuisine.

Chayote: Also known as christophene and choko, this pear-shaped vegetable has a green skin, spiky hairs, and a mild flavor.

Chilies: Many different varieties of chili are used in South and Southeast Asia with varying degrees of heat. As a general rule, the smaller the chili the hotter it is. **Bird's-eye chilies**, which are used in many of these recipes, are tiny red or green chilies and are fiery hot. Whenever using chilies, remove seeds to reduce the heat and wear protective gloves and wash hands well after handling the chilies.

Chinese chive: Also called flat or garlic chive—or *kuchai* throughout much of Southeast Asia—this long, flat chive is fairly pungent and is usually lightly cooked rather than eaten raw.

Chinese key: Known as *krachai* in Thailand where is it most commonly used, Chinese key looks like a cluster of orange-brown fingers. This rhizome is a member of the ginger family and is used either raw or cooked in salads, soups, and curries. Substitute with water-packed *krachai*, sometimes merely labelled "rhizome."

Choy sum: This Chinese flowering cabbage has yellow flowers when mature although it is usually harvested before this stage. The leaves are loosely packed and both the leaves and stems are edible. Substitute with *bok choy* (white, or Chinese, cabbage).

Cilantro: See coriander.

Chinese rice wine: Made from fermented rice, Chinese rice wine is available from supermakets and Asian food stores; you may use dry sherry as a substitute.

Chinese sausage: Made from pork flavored with rose wine, these fatty dried sausages, known as *la chang* in Mandarin and *lap cheong* in Cantonese, are used as a seasoning rather than eaten whole.

Cloves: Indigenous to Indonesia, the dried brown buds of the clove tree are often added whole to curries for flavoring (they are not eaten if used whole).

Coconut milk: In places where fresh coconut is available, the grated flesh of a mature coconut is squeezed with water to obtain coconut milk. Generally, 1/2 cup (125 ml) water is added to 1 coconut and squeezed to obtain thick coconut milk or coconut cream. For thin coconut milk, squeeze the same coconut flesh with 2 1/2 cups (625 ml) water.

Coriander: The seeds, leaves, and roots of the coriander plant are used in South and Southeast Asian cooking. **Cilantro** refers to the fresh leaves and stems.

Crackers: *Krupuk*, as they are known in Malay and Indonesian, are wafers made from prawns, fish, or melinjo nuts. Dry thoroughly before deep-frying in oil when they puff up spectacularly.

Curry leaf: Available fresh or dried from Asian foodstores, the small, dark green curry leaf is popular throughout much of South and Southeast Asia and possesses a unique and very disctinctive fragrance when fried. There is no substitute for this.

Daikon: This giant white radish looks like a large white carrot. Popular in Japan, it may be eaten raw or used in cooked dishes. If raw, *daikon* is usually grated small, sprinkled with salt and left to stand for 10 minutes before being rinsed. The sprouts may also be eaten.

Dashi: Japanese stock made from dried bonito flakes and dried kelp.

Fennel: The seeds, which look like cumin seeds, impart a liquorice or aniseed-like flavor to dishes. Available from Indian foodstores.

Fish sauce: A mainstay of Vietnamese, Thai, and Cambodian cuisine, fish sauce is made from salted, fermented fish or shrimps and is used in much the same way the Chinese use soy sauce.

Galangal: A rhizome of the ginger family, yet with a very different fragrance and taste to ginger. Galangal is pink in color and goes by the name of *laos* in Indonesia, *lengkuas* in Malaysia, and *kha* in Thailand.

Garam masala: A popular blend of spices, used to flavor Indian cooking, which is sold premixed in Asian foodstores.

Green pea shoots: The tender young shoots of snow and sugar peas are prized by Chinese cooks, who refer to them as *dou miao*. Substitute with watercress.

fennel

curry leaf

Chinese keys

aromatic ginger

lentils, black gram

mustard greens, pickled

noodles, rice vermicelli

shrimp paste, dried

ajowan

cardamom

crackers

shrimps, dried

noodles, *kuzukiri*

lime leaf, kaffir

coriander

mushrooms, monkey head

pandan leaf

tofu, deep-fried

basil, sweet

star anise

palm sugar

nutmeg

lime

Sichuan vegetable

tempe

lentils, red & yellow

Vietnamese mint

basil, Thai

Hoisin sauce: A sweet barbecue sauce that may be used as a marinade ingredient or a dipping sauce.

Lemongrass: As its name suggests, this grass posseses a distinctive lemony fragrance. Only the bottom 4 in (10 cm) of the lemongrass bulb should be used; the coarse leaves may be discarded.

Lentils: Three types of lentils are used in these recipes. Red lentils, also called *masoor dal*, are salmon pink in color when husked; black gram lentils (*ulundoo* or *urad dal*) are sold with their black skin on or husked, when they are creamy white; yellow lentils, or *tuvar dal*, are small and pale yellow.

Lime: Three varieties of lime are used in these recipes. The **calamansi** is a very small round lime of medium fragrance and acidity. It is known as *limau kesturi* in Malay and is often used to garnish noodle dishes. Regular round pale green limes are used where lime juice is required; lemon juice may be substituted. The **kaffir lime**—also called fragrant or leprous lime—has a dark green, warty skin and its figure-of-eight leaves are very popular in Southeast Asian cooking. Available fresh or frozen from Asian food-stores, they are known as *bai magrut* in Thai, *daun limau purut* in Malay, and *daun jeruk purut* in Indonesia. The leaves are finely shredded and eaten raw or used in cooked dishes.

Mushrooms: Wipe fresh mushrooms with a paper towel and remove the coarse stems. Monkey head mushrooms, *tou hou gan* in Mandarin, are available from specialist shops and are so-named because of their short, spiky hair which is said to resemeble the hair on a monkey's head. If you cannot find them, substitute with fresh *shiitake* mushrooms.

Noodles: A wide variety of noodles are used in these recipes. They include fresh flat or round (laksa) noodles which can be kept for several days in the refrigerator. Dried rice noodles range in thickness from the thick, flat ribbon noodles to rice sticks and the thin threads of vermicelli. Fresh egg noodles are available in a variety of thicknesses and can be stored for several days if refrigerated. Cellophane, or glass, noodles are made from mung bean starch and come as vermicelli or flat noodles.

Nori: Also known as laver or sloke, this dried seaweed is toasted and used as a wrap for *norimaki* (sushi rolled in *nori*).

Nutmeg: Native to the Spice Islands, nutmeg is used in Western sweets but Asian savory dishes. Dried nutmeg keeps almost indefinitely. On the outside of some nutmeg is mace, a red lacey web or aril which is used predominantly in dishes of Indian origin.

Palm sugar: Made from either the *aren* or coconut palm, it is sold as hard brown cylinders. Substitute with soft brown sugar and a touch of maple syrup.

Pandan leaf: The leaf of the pandanus or screwpine is long, green, and blade-like. It is raked with the tines of a fork or tied in a knot before being added to the pot to impart flavor to savory dishes, used as a wrapping for seasoned morsels of chicken or pork, or it may be pounded to extract the juice to add a touch of green color to sweet dishes.

Paneer: A kind of Indian curd cheese which is made by mixing milk with vinegar to form a curd, draining this curd through a muslin cloth and then leaving to set a few hours covered by a heavy object.

Pickled mustard greens: Salted and preserved mustard greens (*kiam chye*) can be found in Chinese supermarkets.

Saffron: This expensive spice is actually the dried stigma of a type of crocus that grows in Kashmir, and the Mediterranean. Avoid powdered saffron which does not possess an intense taste; store saffron threads in the freezer.

Salam **leaf**: This large, dark green leaf is used in Indonesian cooking where it is added whole to curries for flavor. It is not common in any other Asian cuisine and has no direct substitute; if it is unavailable, simply omit it from the recipe.

Sesame: **Sesame seeds** are roasted and used in numerous Indian dishes as well as Chinese desserts, and have a wonderful nutty aroma. Available from health food-stores and Asian grocers. **Sesame oil** is made from ground roasted sesame seeds. It burns easily and is not often used for stir-frying but is added to dishes at the end of cooking—a drop at a time since its flavor and aroma are so strong.

Shrimp paste, dried: This pungent flavoring is usally sold as crumbly beige to brown or black cakes or squares. Dried shrimp paste must be cooked before eating—either wrap in foil and broil (grill), cook in a dry pan on all sides, or hold over a naked flame on the back of a spoon. Shrimp paste is sold under its Malay name *belacan* (pronounced "blachan") or its Indonesian name *trassi*.

Shrimps, dried: Tiny dried shrimps must be soaked in warm water for five minutes to soften before use. Discard any bits of hard shell that float to the surface.

Sichuan vegetable: Tubers of mustard greens are sun-dried, pickled, pressed, then blended with chili and spices. Also known as preserved vegetable.

Star anise: This anise-flavored, eight-pointed star is a common in Chinese cooking but also shows up in Thai, Malaysian, and Indonesian dishes. It is usually added whole and should not be eaten.

Tamarind: Known as *asam jawa* in Malay and Indonesian, and *ma khaam* in Thai, tamarind imparts a sour flavor to many Southeast Asian dishes. It is usually sold in pulp form. Simply soak the required amount of pulp in water for about five minutes, then squeeze, stir, and strain the liquid to remove all pulp and solids and use the tamarind water as a souring agent. See *asam gelugor*.

Tempe: These cakes of compressed, lightly fermented soya beans have a delicious nutty flavor and are becoming known outside of their origin of Java for their health benefits.

Tiger lily buds: Also known as golden needles, these dried unopened tiger lilies have a crunchy texture and mild taste.

Tofu: The Japanese name for bean curd, tofu, the by-product of soy beans, is popular the world over as a health food. Tofu has no flavor but absorbs the flavor of whatever it is cooked with. Also available pressed (*tau kwa*), dried and deep-fried (*tau pok*), and as dried skin (*foo juk*).

Turmeric: A vivid yellow rhizome of the ginger family, turmeric is available fresh or in powder form. Turmeric leaf is used as a herb in Sumatran cooking and, since there is no direct substitute, omit it from the recipe if not available.

Vietnamese mint, long-stemmed: With stongly flavored, long, arrow-shaped leaves, this is, for many, an essential ingredient in laksa—it is known as *daun* laksa (laksa leaf), or *daun kesom*, in Singapore and Malaysia, *rau ram* in Vietnam, and polygonum in botanical circles.

Wakame: a kind of seaweed often used in Japanese *miso* soup as well as in raw and cooked salads.

Water apple: With only a subtle flavor and hint of sweetness, the water apple is enjoyed more for its crisp juiciness. An excellent choice for all salads.

Water convolvulus: A popular vegetable all over Southeast Asia, the shoots and leaves may be eaten. Most commonly known as *kangkung*.

stockists

Most of the ingredients in this book can be found in markets featuring the foods of South and Southeast Asia, as well as in Chinese and Japanese food-stores, and large supermarkets. Ingredients not found locally may be available from the mail-order markets listed below.

Australia
The Asian Sensation
T: (02) 4472-7939
E: asiansen@sci.net.au
www.ozebiz.com.au/asian

Germany
Asia-Laden
T: (451) 705 221
E: info@asia-laden.de
www.asia-laden.de

Elen's Asia Shop
T: 2154 - 911 236
E: kontakt@elens-asia-shop.de
www.elens-asia-shop.de

India Food Company
T: (40) 381 178
www.india-food.de

Scandinavia
Siagians
E: siagians@geocities.com
www.geocities.com/MadisonAvenue/8074/BetalaE.html

UK
Bristol Sweet Mart
T: (0117) 951 2257
www.sweetmart.co.uk

Duan's Thai Ingredients
E: flanakin@dial.pipex.com
www.flanakin.dial.pipex.com

ChineseStore.co.uk
E:enquiry@chinesestore.co.uk
www.chinesestore.co.uk

USA
A Cook's Wares
T: (412) 846-9490
www.cookswares.com

AsiaFoods.com
E: info@asia.foods.com
www.asiafoods.com

Bachri's Chili & Spice Gourmet
Toll Free (800) 511-6451
E:bachris@telerama.lm.com
users.telerama.com/~bachris

Dean & DeLuca
T: (877) 826-9246
E: atyourservice@deandeluca.com
www.deandeluca.com

Funga Luscious, Inc.
(dried exotic mushrooms)
fungaluscious.freeyellow.com

Import Food
T: (425) 392-7516
E: info@importfood.com
www.importfood.com

IndoStores.com
E: productrequest@indostores.com
www.indostores.com

Penzeys Ltd
T: (800) 741 7787
E: customerservice@penzeys.com
www.penzeys.com

SpiceEtc
T: (800) 827-6373
E: spices@spicesetc.com
www.spicesetc.com

Thai Grocer
T: (773) 988-8424
E: email@thaigrocer.com
www.thaigrocer.com

The CMC Company
T: 800-CMC-2780
E:sales@thecmccompany.com
www.thecmccompany.com

The Oriental Pantry
T: (978) 264-4576
www.orientalpantry.com

The Spice House
T: (847) 328-3711
www.thespicehouse.com

acknowledgments

The recipes in this book were created by:
Four Seasons Resort Bali at Jimbaran Bay Executive Chef Marc Miron
Four Seasons Resort Bali at Sayan Resort Chef Vindex Valentino Tengker
Four Seasons Resort Maldives at Kuda Huraa Executive Chef Frank Ruidavet
Four Seasons Hotel Singapore Executive Chef Martin Awyong Chinese Executive Chef Jereme Leung

The publisher would like to thank Neil Jacobs, the management and staff of Four Seasons Resorts and Hotels Asia Pacific for their generous assistance in the production of this book.

Special thanks to the following shops for the loan of their beautiful tableware and fabrics:
Club21
190 Orchard Boulevard
#01-02 Four Seasons Hotel
Singapore 248646
T: (65) 235-0753
www.clubtwentyone.com
Galeri Esok Lusa
Jl. Raya Basangkasa

47 Seminyak, Kuta, Bali
T: (361) 735-262
E: gundul@idola.net.id
Boutique at Four Seasons Resort Jimbaran Bay
Jenggala Keramik
Jalan Uluwatu II, Jimbaran-Bali
T: (361) 703310
E: info@jenggala-bali.com
www.jenggala-bali.com
John Hardy
Br. Baturning, Mambal, Abiansemal, PO Box 2555
Tonja, Denpasar, Bali
T: (361) 244-311/2
Lotus Arts De Vivre
#01-28 Raffles Hotel Arcade
Raffles Hotel, Singapore 189673
T: (65) 334-2085
E: lotus@lotusartsdevivre.com
www.lotusartsdevivre.com
Narumi Serasi Indah
Jl BY Pass Ngurah Rai No. 77
Komp. Ruko No. 7 , Nusa Dua
T: (361) 775-713
E: narumibl@indosat.net.id
Resort Shop at Four Seasons Resort Maldives
Sayan Shop at Four Seasons Resort Sayan
page credits
19 silver bowl & platter – John Hardy; shell & coral spoons – Lotus Arts De Vivre **20–1** table

setting – Jenggala Keramik; spoon – Boutique (Jimbaran Bay) **23** plate, salt & pepper holders – John Hardy **28** bowl & plate – Jenggala Keramik **37** coaster – Boutique (Jimbaran Bay) **39** two bowls in background – Club21 **40** Jenggala Keramik **46** plate – Jenggala Keramik; mat – Sayan Shop **53** chopsticks – John Hardy **54** platter & napkin holder – Sayan Shop **56** plates – Club21 **60** bamboo & silver tray – John Hardy **72** fabric – Resort Shop (Maldives) **79** jade chopsticks – Lotus Arts De Vivre; condiment set – Club21 **88–9** basket – Resort Shop (Maldives); silver bowl & shell spoon – Lotus Arts De Vivre **90** placemat – Sayan Shop **95** plate – Club21 **97** horn bowl – Club21; gold fililgree chopsticks – Lotus Arts De Vivre **103** platter – Jenggala Keramik; lacquer dish – Sayan Shop **110** bowl – Jenggala Keramik; tray & basket – Sayan Shop **112** cutlery – John Hardy; plate – Narumi Serasi Indah **117** tray – Sayan Shop **119** fork – John Hardy; platter – Narumi Serasi Indah **120** chopsticks & fabric – Resort Shop (Maldives)

122–3 platter – Jenggala Keramik; silver & coconut plate – John Hardy **127** plate – Jenggala Keramik; mat – Sayan Shop **128** plate – Narumi Serasi Indah **132** mat – Sayan Shop **135** bowl & plate – Jenggala Keramik **136** glasses – Jenggala Keramik **139** platter – Jenggala Keramik **140** plate – Jenggala Keramik **143** silver & wood tray – John Hardy **147** placemat – Resort Shop (Maldives) **151** platter – Galeri Esok Lusa **154–5** plate – Jenggala Keramik; fabric, trays & chopsticks – Sayan Shop **157** saucers – Jenggala Keramik **158** shell & silver servers – Lotus Arts De Vivre **166** plate – Galeri Esok Lusa **169** chopsticks – Jenggala Keramik **170–1** plates – Jenggala Keramik; tray – Sayan Shop **174** Jenggala Keramik **177** tray – Boutique (Jimbaran Bay) **178** plate – Jenggala Keramik; tray – Sayan Shop **181** bowl – Jenggala Keramik; cutlery – Boutique (Jimbaran Bay)

Thanks also to Mrs Ong Kiat Kim, Yaeko Masuda, and Mag Ong.

index